This book is the property of

_____

EMOTIONS FOR TEENS AND TWEENS

The first visual book on emotional intelligence for tweens and teens told through infographics. A graphic guide to understanding, managing, expressing feelings, and building relationships

Boulder, CO

Contents

Chapter 3. I Feel…

Chapter 4. Getting Along With Your Feelings

Chapter 5. What Do Others Feel?

Why Should I Read This Book?

"Irritation, anger, resentment, boredom, embarrassment... They come and go as they please. They fill me to the brim and make me say and do things that I will be ashamed of. People say, 'Pull yourself together,' or 'Control your emotions.' How can I do that? Should I just keep silent and frown, like my Dad? Or should I yell like my sister?"

"Sometimes I simply don't understand what I am feeling. There is an emptiness inside me that makes me cold. Other times my emotions are so abundant that I want to run and hide. Lately it has become especially difficult to cope with them. Mom asks, 'What's going on with you?' And I simply have no idea what to answer...
What exactly are emotions? Why do they take charge? How can I learn to live with them?"

With this book in hand, try to find answers to all these questions. We promise — the book understands you. Every page will help you get to know yourself a bit better, give you tips on what you feel, or reveal the secret of how to control your emotions. It will also tell you what other people are feeling. Chances are that if you pay attention to what you read, even your parents will soon ask you for advice.

This is not your usual book.
It doesn't have a lot of text, but it has a lot of meaning.
It covers serious topics, but in an exciting and captivating manner. It uses a lot of pictures, which older people like to call infographics (to avoid telling you they love pictures, too). You can read it from front to back, or you can simply turn to the topic that you're preoccupied with right now.

Alright, let's figure out what feelings you're having, shall we?

CHAPTER 1
What Exactly Are Feelings?

- Feelings and Emotions: What Are They?

- Why Do We Need Feelings?

- How Do Feelings Emerge?

- Am I the Sum of My Feelings and Emotions?

- Do Emotions Boost Your Energy?

- *What's Next?*

Feelings and Emotions: What Are They?

Things happens to us every day, and we respond to these experiences. We get happy, sad, angry, afraid, or curious. Overall, we go through a multitude of feelings and emotions. Even when we do nothing, we feel something!

What is the difference?

EMOTIONS

The way you react to something that irritates you. Emotion is like a musical note, it makes a sound for a short while and disappears quickly.
An emotion is usually reflected instantly in your facial expressions and body language.

FEELINGS

The way you feel about something or someone for an extended period of time. Feelings are like a melody made of many notes. They may live in us for years.

How are they connected?

As a rule, emotions emerge for a reason. The reason for your emotional response is often hidden in some feeling. And feelings, in turn, consist of many complex emotions. They may even become sources of emotions.

For example, a classmate came up with a stupid nickname for you and shouted it out in class. It was very awkward for you and even a bit sad, and your face turned completely red.

These are emotions

For example, you are the new kid in school, and you feel insecure and afraid that your classmates will not accept you. That's why you're even slumping in your chair a bit.

These are feelings

Knowing this difference makes it easier to understand what you feel in a specific moment.

What causes our feelings and emotions?

OCCURRENCES
Everything that happens around you may influence you. It could be any random thing, even a change in the weather!

PEOPLE
Everyone around you has an influence on you, from a chance meeting to communication you have with your friends and family.

THOUGHTS
Everything you think about is closely connected to your emotions. For instance, you may recall some occurrence and you start feeling happy or embarrassed. Or you may start thinking about things you need to do and get anxious.

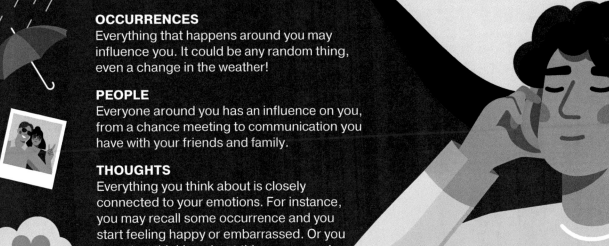

What is affected by feelings and emotions?

Your perception of occurrences
If you're in a good mood, you're unlikely to get worked up over your ice cream cone falling on the floor. But if you're having a bad day, you will react as if it is the ultimate insult.

Your perception of people
A classmate has decided to give you a present. If you like that person, you will happily accept his or her present and think what a great friend you have. But if you're not comfortable with this guy or girl, you might think he or she's trying to butter you up or has a hidden agenda.

Your perception of yourself
Let's say you've quarreled with a friend, and you blame yourself for this situation. Now you feel like you're a bad friend. But if you think you're not the only one at fault, then you won't consider yourself a bad friend.

Ask yourself: what has influenced you today? And what effect have your emotions had on your surroundings?
By learning to see this connection, you will have a better understanding of what drives your actions and feelings.

Emotions and feelings can be barely noticeable, just like a subtle sound, or they can be extremely loud, like a full orchestra.

When an orchestra plays, you definitely take notice. It may play out of tune, or the sound is too loud or unpleasant, in which case these types of feelings are difficult to deal with, and you may want to run for shelter. But there's nowhere to run, as all of this is happening inside of your head.

It's entirely different with low-profile, but long-lasting feelings. They can easily go unnoticed, but they can make a strong impact on your perceptions and state of mind.

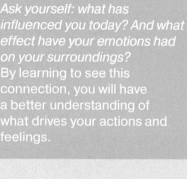

Does everybody have the same feelings?

Psychologist Paul Ekman spent years studying human emotions and experimenting. He highlighted six basic emotions, with which many other scientists tend to agree.

Try to recreate Ekman's experiment and name the emotions expressed in the faces below.

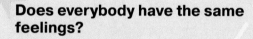
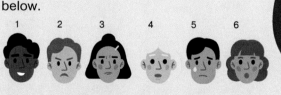

According to Ekman, these emotions are the core of all other emotions and feelings. Yes, there are only six basic emotions, and you can easily tell them by facial expressions.

At the same time, everybody feels so many variations of these emotions, and root causes of their feelings are so different that it's safe to say that your feelings and emotions are unique.

1. Joy. 2. Anger. 3. Disgust. 4. Fear. 5. Sadness. 6. Surprise.

Using the analogy above, what are the loudest emotions you have felt over the past few days? And what are the quieter ones?

Rate each of them on a scale of 1 to 10, where 10 is very loud!

Why Do We Need Feelings?

You meet somebody and you soon realize that you feel comfortable with this person, that you want to stay in touch with him or her. How were you able to determine this if you have only known each other for a mere 10 minutes? In this instance, your feelings and emotions serve as your superpowers and allow you to perceive the world and respond instantly to what is happening both around and inside you.

RATIONAL INTELLIGENCE
Its purpose is for thinking. Beyond that, it helps you learn, memorize, gain experience, and then put it to use.

Researchers discovered that two systems work in our heads simultaneously: one is **rational**, and the other is **emotional**.

How did our ancestors develop feelings?

Basic positive and negative emotions helped primitive people survive.

More complex feelings such as love, sadness, and happiness helped them communicate with each other. After all, it's much safer and more pleasant and exciting to live among people of your own kind.

Why do we need rational intelligence?

We would have never invented the wheel, come up with the law of levers, or designed the smartphone in your hand were it not for rational intelligence. Without it, we would not be able to dream or make plans. And we would have a much harder time living together. For anything we do collectively requires that we be able to reach an agreement or at least possess the ability to understand each other without words!

The two types of intelligence work together and are very efficient at it!

What do our feelings actually do?

1 **They send signals to draw our attention to something or someone.**

All clear!
Positive emotions comfort and inspire us when we move in the right direction.

Danger!
Negative emotions scream if there is an external threat, or if we do something wrong.

2 **They help us make decisions**
Every day our emotions tell us what option to choose out of a multitude of possibilities. Even when you believe that your decision was totally based on logic, emotions still played an important part in this process.

3 **They help us communicate**
You understand easily what other people feel based on their facial expressions, posture, and voices. If we were not able to understand other people's emotions, it would be impossible to communicate with them!

EMOTIONAL INTELLIGENCE
It enables you to understand yourself as well as others. What's more, you instantaneously react to events well before you were able to figure out what has actually occured.

Danger? All clear!

How do danger signals work these days? They are a bit behind the times. For instance, you hear something rustling in a bush next to your house. You know for sure that it's not a predator. But your brain still signals danger and turns on your fear and anxiety.

The same goes for your imagination: you are afraid of spiders, fire, ghosts, or being alone, even if there is no apparent danger.

All clear? Danger!

Imagine yourself in Africa 200,000 years ago. If you heard a rustling in a nearby bush, you certainly would have felt intense fear and run away since there was definitely a dangerous predator hiding there. This strategy worked well for survival, didn't it?

Why do we feel danger even if there isn't any?

Basic instinctive emotions are managed by our reptilian brain, the oldest part of the brain (located in the occipital lobe). It works now just the same as it worked among our ancestors. We can't stop receiving signals from our reptilian brain even with the help of our neocortex (frontal lobe), the youngest part of the present-day human brain.

But you can pacify these signals: when you feel fear or anxiety for no reason, try to imagine that they were caused by some timid lizard in your head. You can picture yourself patting it on the back, comforting it, convincing it that there's no reason to be afraid.

How Do Feelings Emerge?

Feelings result from a complex combination of our past experience, our current situation, and the way this is all processed by the brain. The condition your nervous and hormonal system are in also plays a part. Even though scientists have still not reached consensus on this, there are indeed some things we already know.

BRAIN — BODY HIGHWAY

The spinal cord, being the primary connector, transmits information about your body to and from the brain and passes on instructions from the brain to all the body's organs.

SENSORY ORGANS

These are our conductors to the outside world. Everything that happens around you reaches your brain through your sense of sight, touch, sound, smell, and spatial orientation.

ROADS AND PATHWAYS

There is an extensive network of billions of threads inside you that is called the nervous system. It consists of cells called neurons and the connections between them. This network works nonstop: impulses constantly carry information about everything that is happening both inside and outside of you and transmit it from neuron to neuron.

MASTER CONTROL

Your brain is the birthplace of dreams, ideas, emotions and feelings. The brain gets signals and gives instructions through other areas of the nervous system.

How do we understand the world?

The brain controls our body, reactions, thoughts, and feelings. It has an enormous responsibility and mission that can only be completed with the help of 'agents', meaning elements of the nervous system. What's more, the brain constantly hypothesizes about events, using past experiences as a reference.

1 The brain receives signals from both inside and outside of the body.

2 It hypothesizes about what is going on, based on past experiences and new data.

3 It instructs the nervous system how it must react.

4 It verifies whether or not the hypothesis is correct. If not, it adjusts its instructions and commits to memory the new experience.

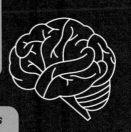

AUTOPILOT

The nervous system is responsible for everything that happens in your body. How your heart beats, your blood circulates, your digestive system processes food, and your lungs breathe. It consists of several divisions, each having its own mission.

CHEMICAL FACTORY

The endocrine system helps the nervous system regulate how your body functions. It is comprised of different organs in all parts of your body, which discharge chemical substances called hormones. These hormones control growth, pubertal development, organ performance, and even your state of mind. The hormone system and its condition may strongly influence your emotions and feelings.

ACCELERATE

The sympathetic nervous system, or the 'fight or flight' system, is responsible for reacting to any signal. It helps us function, solve problems, and be active.

BRAKE

The parasympathetic system is responsible for leisure and the digestion response. It helps us relax and accumulate energy and strength for our next leap.

IDEALLY THE ACCELERATOR AND BRAKE SHOULD BE UTILIZED IN BALANCE WITH ONE ANOTHER

This will give you enough time to relax, so that you will not react to irritants too strongly. If you accelerate too often and always maintain a high rate of speed, then your emotions and reactions will be over the top.

Example: A friend has postponed your get-together, which is no big deal in itself, but you're already on the verge of tears.

Can you control your nervous and endocrine systems?

Not much. Science thinks they operate on their own, and they are essential to the proper functioning of your body.

But scientists have proved that we can consciously aid them.

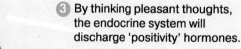

1 By maintaining a balance between leisure and activity.

2 By taking care of your health.

3 By thinking pleasant thoughts, the endocrine system will discharge 'positivity' hormones.

What if you know nothing about your feelings?

The brain thinks big. Imagine a person who has never heard of happiness, fear, love, or other feelings. She only thinks in terms of good and bad. This person won't be able to figure out what is happening to her, what she is feeling, or what she can do about it, because she doesn't have the proper experience to develop the correct hypothesis about what is going on. That's why it's important to know what feelings you may come across!

BAD

GOOD

Am I the Sum of My Feelings and Emotions?

A ship without a captain can never reach its destination: during stormy weather waves will toss it onto the rocks, or the windless calm will keep it sailing idly. The same happens to humans who are not in tune with their emotions.

Emotions and feelings are just a part of your 'self', but are a very important part, perhaps being at times the most important aspect of your life. But you can learn to differentiate between yourself and your feelings.

FEELINGS

EMOTIONS

THOUGHTS

SENSES

Where is your location?

YOU ARE AN OBSERVER WHEN

- You realize what is happening to you and your body.
- You understand why you are feeling a certain way.
- You accept your emotions, and don't reject them.
- You know that all your emotions are important.
- You understand that you can get through it all.

WHEN YOU ARE CONTROLLED BY EMOTIONS

- You are unable to grasp what is happening to you and your body.
- You act impulsively.
- You can't take an unbiased look at your situation.
- You are critical of yourself.
- You suppress your emotions, or you run rampant.

WHEN YOU LEARN TO OBSERVE YOURSELF, YOU WILL BE ABLE TO LIVE CONSCIOUSLY AND IN HARMONY WITH YOUR FEELINGS

What is consciousness?

- Being in tune with the current moment, having the ability to live in the now.
- Being aware of and understanding your body.
- Being aware of and understanding your emotions.
- Being aware of and understanding your thoughts.

Tips to Master Your Wheel and Be Conscious of Your Emotions

1 MEASURING YOUR EMOTIONS

Make it a habit to measure your current condition with the help of the mood meter, the creation of Yale Professor Marc Brackett.

HOW DO I USE THE MOOD METER?

Measure your mood and energy and determine which section of the meter is a better representation of your condition.

This will help you:

1 Measure your current condition.

2 Figure out which activity will suit you best at a particular moment.

ENERGY

MOOD

Bad mood, lots of energy:
Clean the house.
Engage in your hobby.
Compete in something.

Good mood, lots of energy:
Do something athletic.
Come up with new ideas.
Take a walk with friends.
Take up something you've been postponing for a long time.

Bad mood, low energy:
Get support.
Take care of yourself.
Do something pleasant.
Read your list of happy moments.

Good mood, low energy:
Read.
Watch a movie.
Learn something new.
Communicate with friends.

2 RECOLLECTING

This is a simple exercise that helps build up consciousness. Recall a situation that has happened to you recently.

Desired reaction
How would you like to react to that situation?

Actual reaction
How did you actually react?

Emotional cause
What emotions were you experiencing? What feelings caused this reaction?

After you have answered these questions, it will be easier for you to switch to the observer mode next time.

3 PAUSE

Our first response to a situation is often very emotional and ill-considered. It is especially difficult to switch to the observer mode when you are overwhelmed with negative feelings. But there is a life-hack that will help you slow down.

You respond to a situation by feeling a wave of anger, fury, profound sadness or something that puts you off your stride.

Pause and take three to five deep breaths.

Now you can feel your blood rushing through your veins a bit more slowly, and you can concentrate on something for a few seconds.

This latest emotional wave did not overwhelm you because you had time to transition and your brain was able to adjust its hypothesis about possible developments and called off the 'alarm.'

Do Emotions Boost Your Energy?

Our feelings can be a source of energy. But they can also deprive us of it. If you learn to nurture some emotions and let go of others, your goals will be much easier to reach.

What fuels us?

Energy is our primary life source. When we have a lot of energy, we are vibrant and ready to be achievers. When we are low on energy, we don't feel like doing anything. It's important to learn to maintain a balance between activity and leisure.

It's also important to remember that all energy types are interconnected and to be able to balance them.

Energy types

PHYSICAL ENERGY
Fuel for other energy types. If you spend all your days motionless in front of your computer, it should come as no surprise that you feel down and have no desire to take on new tasks.

EMOTIONAL ENERGY
Both positive and negative emotions are needed for energy balance. They consume and generate energy. They are directly connected to physical activity and the realization of your best abilities.

MENTAL ENERGY
It helps you to meet any challenges you might face. It fades away quickly in the absence of action or nutrition. It may seem that you don't understand something, while it's often simply the result of your batteries being low.

SPIRITUAL ENERGY
Taking care of yourself and other people. Be kind, loving, and warm-hearted — these are very powerful energy sources.

Why am I too lazy to get things done?

Laziness is not a personality trait, but rather a signal that may have various causes, e.g. fear or a lack of energy or motivation.

How can you recharge your batteries?

0%

You're tired and unwilling to do anything.
When you haven't taken a break for a long time, and your efforts haven't given you any enjoyment, you get burned out. Your top priority at the moment is to **charge your batteries**. Postpone all your activities for a few days or even a week. Sleep until noon, take a walk in the forest, watch movies, stay away from your phone. Tell your family what you're going through.

30%

You feel like doing something, but you have no energy. Your top priority at the moment is to **cheer up**. You need rest, but not as long as when your energy is at zero. Take a walk, read a book or watch a movie, dream for a while. Add some physical activity.

60%

You feel like doing something, and you have the energy, but now and again you get distracted and postpone things until later.
Your top priority at the moment is to **bring your energy up to a productive level**. Anything that cheers you up and empowers you will do: eat a chocolate bar, chat with friends, or go jogging. These small pleasant things will quickly boost your energy.

I don't feel like doing anything!

FEAR AND ANXIETY
You're afraid that you might not be up to the task. Or an activity is unfamiliar to you and you don't know what to expect.

SOLUTION:
- Put together a detailed plan, breaking down your overall task into subtasks.
- Recall your prior achievements and imagine how easily you will pull this one off, too.

LOW ENERGY
Your body gives you a signal that its energy is too low for any major undertaking.

SOLUTION:
- Recharge your batteries by doing what you enjoy doing and get some rest.
- Switch over to a smaller undertaking for a while.

LOW MOTIVATION
You're not taking up an activity because it's not what you want to do, or you're not interested in doing it.

SOLUTION:
- Find an aspect of an activity that you do enjoy, and focus on that aspect.
- If you regularly have to do something unfulfilling, think about ways to replace this activity with an exciting one.

YOU PUT OFF THE INEVITABLE
You always find something else to do just to avoid doing what is truly important.

SOLUTION:
- Put together a strict daily regimen.
- Set a timer for 15 to 20 minutes and focus on just one activity without any distractions. Follow this with a 10-minute break.

What's Next?

Things to keep in mind

- What are you feeling? Are you able to discern whether this is a single emotion or a complex feeling that consists of several emotions?

- Is there a feeling that has been in you for a long time? What is it? How does it influence your life?

- Recall your recent choices, even insignificant ones. Were they driven by rational thought or by emotion?

- When does your rational intelligence help you more often, and when does your emotional intelligence take over?

- When was the last time that your desired reaction to an event was the same as your actual reaction? And when was your reaction totally different from the desired one? What was the reason?

Worth reading

- Paul Ekman. **Emotions Revealed: Recognizing Faces and Feelings to Improve Communication and Emotional Life**

- Daniel Goleman. **Emotional Intelligence: Why it Can Matter More Than IQ**

- Ilse Sand. **The Emotional Compass**

Worth watching

Tiffany Watt Smith.
The history of human emotions

Sophie Zadeh.
Are there universal expressions of emotion?

CHAPTER 2
How Do I Know What I Am Feeling?

- I Don't Understand What I Am Feeling

- Your Body Is a Mirror of Your Emotions

- Can Emotions Be 'Good' and 'Bad'?

- Is It Possible To Only Experience Pleasant Feelings?

- *What's Next?*

I Don't Understand What I Am Feeling

"What am I feeling, and why do I feel this way?" This is a tough question. Let's try and study the flower of our emotions together, like curious natural scientists would do. This model, designed by U.S. scientist Robert Plutchik, works great for this purpose.

How does the flower of emotions work?

The strongest emotions are in the center of the flower. The farther an emotion is from the center, the weaker it is.

- ● **RAGE**
- ● **ANGER**
- ● **ANNOYANCE**

Feelings that emerge as a combination of several emotions are listed on petals in between the main petals.

- ● **SADNESS**
  +
- ● **DISGUST**
  =
- ● **REMORSE**

Petals located on the other side of the flower from one another are direct opposites.

- ● **GRIEF**
- ● **ECSTASY**

serenity

optimism

interest

joy

anticipation

ecstasy

aggressive-ness

vigilance

annoyance

anger

rage

loathing

contempt

grief

disgust

boredom

sadness

remorse

pensive-ness

Why study your emotions?

YOU WILL HAVE A BETTER UNDERSTANDING OF YOURSELF AND OTHER PEOPLE

Every person feels something and behaves under the influence of his or her feelings. After you have figured out what you are feeling, you will have a better understanding of yourself and the people around you.

YOU WILL HAVE BETTER CONTROL OVER YOUR EMOTIONS

After you have learned to understand the causes of your feelings and are able to foresee your reaction, you will obtain the key to controlling your emotions and actions.

love

accept-ance

trust

admira-tion

submission

terror

fear

appre-hension

amaze-ment

awe

surprise

distraction

disapproval

What questions should I ask?

Study the list of emotions and ask yourself:

What am I feeling?

On which petal is my emotion located?

How strong is it?

What has happened?

What actions does this emotion push me toward?

In what other way can I react?

How would I like to feel in this situation?

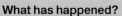

Your Body Is a Mirror of Your Emotions

When we are afraid, sad, or happy, and when we feel loved or rejected, our body is the first responder. It often understands what is happening earlier than we do and sends us signals. Let's decode them.

TEMPERATURE OF EMOTIONS
Joyful, carefree feelings are often perceived as **warmth** inside the **body**. Unpleasant, burdensome feelings produce the sensation of coldness.

Identifying a sensation

Keep a diary of your sensations on a daily basis. Record an emotion and the sensations you feel in your body, as well as the occurrence that influenced your condition. Compare your records to previous days and be on the lookout for similar sensations.

Establishing a body-feeling connection

PALMS
They get covered in cold sweat when your agitation level is very high.

Stop for two minutes once a day to ask yourself, "What sensation is my body experiencing? Which body part is experiencing the strongest sensations? Why?"

When you're experiencing a strong emotion, ask yourself, "Where do I feel it most of all? Which emotions manifest themselves in this way?"

From time to time, just let yourself feel that your body is alive: your feet are planted firmly on the ground, your hands sense the air moving through your fingers, and there is a tickling sensation in your nose when you breathe.

What do you do about a strong sensation?

1 Focus on the sensation and identify it.

2 Name the emotion that has caused it.

3 Tell yourself, "It's OK, this sensation won't last."

HEAD
It aches when you're stressed or anxious.

CHEEKS
Infatuation, shame, or other strong emotions make your cheeks become flushed.

CHEST
This is where the strongest emotions are reflected. Heat rises in your chest when you're joyful or in love, while misery and sadness cause cold and pain. Anxiety feels like a stone put over your heart. Fear is similar to falling into a void.

MOUTH AND THROAT
Anger and indignation manifest themselves through pain (a lump) in your throat and through the grinding of your teeth.

STOMACH
When you're infatuated, it feels like butterflies are fluttering in your stomach. When you're anxious, you develop a hunger-like sensation. Fear may cause you abdominal pain.

Is it necessary to think about these sensations all the time?

No, but you should learn to notice them. When you recognize certain sensations, you open the door to understanding your emotions. It's up to you to decide when and how deeply you want to dive into these sensations. The most important thing is to be aware of them as much as possible.

Can feelings cause an illness?

Do you often experience headaches or stomach pain, which doctors have been unable to diagnose? This is when you may hear the term 'psychosomatics'. This word means that long-lasting negative emotions can have a direct impact on your health.

What exactly is psychosomatics?

You are distressed by something over a long period of time.

Cortisol, or a stress hormone, is produced in your body nonstop.

They send you a signal by causing you pain.

Your body or certain organs are constantly under stress.

Stomach pains or headaches, skin rashes or allergies — these are the most frequent manifestations of long-lasting distress. If doctors are unable to find the cause of your illness, you should think about whether there is a significant emotional experience you are hiding deep inside.

Can Emotions Be 'Good' and 'Bad'?

Why is it so easy to get angry, and why is it more difficult to get excited? Is it possible to get by without any 'bad' emotions?

Positive and negative emotions

No feelings are 'bad' or 'good', yet they are all necessary and important. But there are indeed pleasant and unpleasant emotions.

PLEASANT EMOTIONS
(we like the sensations they are connected to)

Curiosity

Ecstasy   Joy

Happiness   Love

Enthusiasm

UNPLEASANT EMOTIONS
(they cause sensations that we don't like)

Sadness   Fear   Irritation

Anger   Shame   Disappointment

Hatred   Insult   Doubt

What are the benefits?

UNPLEASANT	PLEASANT
Emotions that cause you discomfort to draw your attention:	Emotions that revitalize and motivate you:
• Warn you of danger. • Make you aware of a problem. • Temporarily invigorate you. • Focus your attention on a task.	• Encourage you to take action. • Help you learn new things and allow you to retain more information. • Invigorate you in the longer term. • Make you healthier.

Why do we experience more unpleasant emotions and seem to benefit less from them?

It was crucial for mankind's survival that our ancestors learn to notice danger and react to it quickly. **Unpleasant emotions gave us this superpower.** These emotions serve as large bells that send signals of any danger, even if it's imagined.

That is why we react more strongly to fear than surprise, to insults than gratitude. Times have changed, but this mechanism, tried-and-tested over centuries, still holds true — we get worried, become concerned and continue looking for reasons to be bitter as this is how we protect ourselves.

The more often you feel pleasant emotions, the easier you will overcome complicated situations in life and deal with unpleasant emotions.

I want to experience only happiness

If you try to fence yourself off from feelings that may cause you discomfort or deny the anger or bitterness you feel inside, while suppressing shame, this will only result in your not experiencing any feelings at all; you will in effect 'turn to stone'. **Opposites make the world go round.** If there was no black, we would not see white. If there was no misery, we would stop feeling joy.
Take notice of these opposites. Welcome any of their manifestations, as they all give you priceless human experiences.

Why constantly staying positive is not the way to go

You deny life as it is.

You lose the ability to experience a complete set of emotions.

You accumulate unpleasant emotions that eat you up inside, but will inevitably burst out.

You don't share your problems with your friends and family and allow them to help you.

You don't allow yourself to accumulate experience and therefore cannot draw conclusions from it.

I keep focusing on the bad

This is called **negative thinking**, which each of us has inherited from our primitive ancestors as a protective mechanism. Thanks to such negative thinking, we can foresee issues and learn from our mistakes, but as a result we may stop seeing the good in life due to this constant negativity.

How can I notice more of the good things in life?

Pay closer attention to life's pleasant moments. Take some time in the evening to put together a list of five highlights from your day for which you are thankful.

When you have the urge to see an event in a negative light, imagine that you are taking off your glasses with negatively tainted lenses and instead putting on transparent glasses. Then try to describe the same event once again, but this time search for positive aspects.

If you're constantly focusing on negative moments from your past, stop this thought process. Imagine letting these moments flow away down a river until you can no longer see them. Then recall what you have achieved.

What do you do about 'good' and 'bad' feelings?

Accept any feelings and just live with them. Acknowledge their right to exist. Keep them in sight. Maintain a balance: too many unpleasant experiences, just like nonstop joy, signal that the balance has been upset.

Is It Possible To Only Experience Pleasant Feelings?

Not possible. Not gonna happen. That's the answer, loud and clear. Now let's try to figure out what we really mean by saying all feelings are equally necessary and important. And how we can learn to embrace each and every one of them!

What happens if an emotion is switched off?

Imagine getting a gadget that can turn off any emotion for good.

GRIEF AND SADNESS
Let's say your crush doesn't feel the same way about you, and you switch off your sadness. You will no longer have fond recollections of this person and all the pleasant moments that you have had with him or her disappear, meaning you will no longer value him or her. However, you cannot feel the joy of being together if you don't know the sadness of being alone. What's more, people will notice your indifference and start avoiding contact with you.

FEAR
Jumping off a bridge into a river? No problem! Talking to strangers at night? No biggie? Having no fear does not make us brave, but rather makes us fearless. Something bad is sure to happen to such people as fear is a protective mechanism. Turning off fear will also shut down our survival instinct and the pride we gain from overcoming our fears.

SHAME
Being a jerk to other people gives you a rush. Others say that you are always cruel to them, but you don't seem to care. If you don't feel shame, you lose track of your values and principles, both your own and those of society. Such behavior will quickly turn you into a lonesome outcast.

ANGER
Have you been betrayed? Oh well. Have you been yelled at for no good reason? What can you do? Somebody wants to smack you? There's nothing anyone can do about it. If you don't feel anger, you will never figure out how you deserve to be treated. You will never garner enough energy to step up and protect yourself and others.

 Try to imagine what happens if you switch off other emotions!

They go together

Joy will wane if there's no sadness. You will not understand what tranquility is if you've never been stressed, much in the same manner we welcome spring after a long winter. Only when **comparing one feeling with another can a person experience an emotion** to the fullest. By switching off unpleasant feelings, you deprive yourself of experiencing any pleasant feelings.

Feelings vs. brain

Your prefrontal cortex, or prefrontal lobe (the master of all controls), will be fully developed only by the time you turn 20+, but your limbic system (answering for strong emotions) and reptilian brain (responsible for instincts) are completely operational well before that. That's why you're at the stage now when **every feeling you have is like an explosion**. In 10 years, your emotions will calm down a bit, and past experiences will teach you to tone down your reactions. So enjoy this ability while you have it! Experience emotion freely and store memories of your most vivid emotions.

How can you take care of your feelings?

Self-compassion is an excellent tool that will help you enjoy any emotion.

SELF-ESTEEM VS. SELF-COMPASSION

Self-esteem is the opinion you have of yourself based on your achievements. You may think you're cool after scoring the winning goal in a pivotal game, or you may consider yourself worthless after your parents came down hard on you for something you did.

Self-compassion can't be impacted by anything or anyone. This is your personal patronus, a magic spell that is always by your side to help you when you're down.

Never compare yourself to anyone else. You are a unique individual.

Love yourself just because you exist. Regard your errors and achievements as priceless experiences. Don't take shots at yourself (has taking shots ever helped anyone?). Treat yourself as your own best friend and find the right words of encouragement.

Observe yourself consciously. Pay attention to all your feelings without criticizing or admonishing yourself.

What's Next?

Things to keep in mind

- How are strong emotions reflected in your body? How do you experience sadness, joy, fear, and love?

- What do you notice more often — good things or bad things?

- How often do you do something pleasant for yourself?

- What pleases your friend, mom, dad, or brother? What gets them down?

Worth reading

- Kristin Neff. **Self-Compassion. The Proven Power of Being Kind to Yourself**

- Susan David. **Emotional Agility**

- Anna Black. **A Year Of Living Kindfully**

Your tools

- Robert Plutchik's flower of emotions

- Five reasons to be grateful for the day

Worth watching

Ron Gutman.
The hidden power of smiling

Sharon Horesh Bergquist.
How stress affects your body

CHAPTER 3
I Feel...

I Feel Anger

Your teachers don't allow you to use your smartphone in class. A classmate rudely cuts you off during a conversation. Your parents want to take you to the countryside, while your friends are expecting you to hang out with them in the city. "This is driving me mad!" — is what you want to shout at the world. Are you angry? Let's see.

How do I know if I'm angry?

SENSATIONS

Clenched teeth, your hands are tense, your breathing is accelerated, your heart is pounding, your voice is cracking.

THOUGHTS

I'm furious, I'm surrounded by enemies, I hate everyone, myself included.

ACTIONS

You break things, you yell and call others or yourself names, you bicker, you hurt yourself or others.

What kinds of anger are there?

ANNOYANCE
Minor anger may emerge several times a day without an obvious cause if you're tired, sick, you haven't had enough sleep, or if your spirits are down.

FURY
Intense anger that is manifested in a person's face and voice. It's difficult to hide. Fury can be the product of accumulated annoyance.

RAGE
Overwhelming anger that is impossible to control. It's like a dragon that has just woken up and is ready to burn down everything in its path.

Is anger beneficial or destructive?

Just like any emotion, anger is definitely beneficial. But you might think that good people should never get angry. This is a dangerous misconception. Don't pretend that you never experience anger. If you don't accept this emotion, anger will emerge frequently, trying to defend its right to exist, while draining your energy and creating problems for you. Our reaction to anger and the way we behave when we're angry can be helpful and dangerous, both to ourselves and those around us.

ANGER IS DANGEROUS WHEN:

you are out of control
you feel the urge to do something that you will regret later
you lose all your energy and burn out
you become quick-tempered and aggressive

ANGER IS HELPFUL WHEN:

- you pay attention to something really important
- you become more self-confident
- you feel your physical and emotional strength growing
- you are able to protect yourself and others

What happens if you continuously suppress your anger?

Accumulated anger puts you in a constant state of misery and hatred. Doctors believe that suppressed anger may even result in heart, stomach, and skin conditions.

If your inner dragon has awoken

Stop
If you start to yell, take a break; if you raise your hand to strike someone, put it down. Take three deep breaths, and do a mental count: one dragon, two dragons, three dragons… ten dragons.

Think
What are you doing, what have you just done, and what were you just about to do? Ask yourself: "What am I feeling? Aren't these actions only driven by emotions?"

Sense your body
Where exactly are you feeling anger? Does it feel like your blood is boiling, and a drum is beating in your chest?

Examine anger and its causes
Ask yourself again, "Am I really feeling anger? How intense is it? What has woken up my inner dragon?" Measure your anger on a scale of 1 to 10.

Act again!
Find ways to express your anger that are safe for you and others. Say this outloud, "I am very angry at the moment." Such words will not offend anyone, but they will make your feelings clear to other people. Be active. Do something useful, like tidying up your room or going out for jog.

I (Don't) Feel Joy

Joy is the most desired emotion which brings us happiness. But sometimes it gets lost somewhere along the way. "Nothing gives me joy anymore!" — words like these can often be heard from teenagers whose moods are like the weather, constantly changing.
Let's go on the hunt for joy together!

How do I know when I am feeling joy?

SENSATIONS

You feel a surge of energy, an ease of movement, you're relaxed, there's a smile on your face, and you feel tingling in your fingertips.

THOUGHTS

It's been a great day! I'm OK! Life is good! I'm happy!

ACTIONS

You sing, dance, and have fun, you help others, and do everything that you usually don't do when you're sad or bored.

Unnecessary joy

Some ways of experiencing joy only bring you additional problems.
Think about it: do you really need joy like this?

Thrill-seeking entertainment generates an adrenaline rush, but at the same time, it entails serious risks. It gives you joy for just a fleeting moment.

Drugs and alcohol cause short-term euphoria that is quickly followed by disappointment, despondency, and a poor physical state.

Social domination: experiencing a moment of supremacy that you achieve through subduing and humiliating others will eventually scare everyone away from you.

The three emotions of happiness

SATISFACTION
Inner tranquility, when all you want to do is to smile and enjoy life.

JOY
A more intense experience that makes you not only want to smile and laugh, but also to do something good for yourself and others.

EUPHORIA
A very intense and overpowering, but short experience, when a person forgets everything in the world and feels like the happiest person on earth.

Tips to turning on joy

There are several ways how you can help yourself start feeling joy.

The little things
Recall the things that give you joy and satisfaction and repeat them.

Positive plans
Envision your upcoming achievements and successes, enjoy the prospect of becoming a better version of yourself.

New activities
Try doing something new that will bring you the joy of discovery and pleasant surprises.

Contacts with friends and nature
Meet with friends, take walks in the park, observe nature, get to know new people, and try to do all this more frequently.

Altruism
Our helping others makes us and them happier, because altruism is contagious.

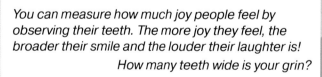

You can measure how much joy people feel by observing their teeth. The more joy they feel, the broader their smile and the louder their laughter is!
How many teeth wide is your grin?

What spoils your joy?

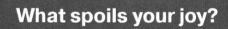

YOU STOP NOTICING THE GOOD THINGS

YOU EXPECT TOO MUCH FROM A PERSON OR EVENT

YOU FOCUS ON THE DOWNSIDE

If you want to be happy, don't compare yourself with or be envious of others. Focus on your own goals and dreams.

Waves of joy
They spread in groups of people. This is called emotional contagion. When you're bored or heavy-hearted, hang out with your friends. Joy can increase in numbers when it is multiplied by good company!

I Am Ashamed and I Blame Myself

A teacher made a negative example of you. Someone cracked a nasty joke about your haircut. And the promise you made to your parents turned out to be too hard to keep. These are three emotions — discomfort, guilt, and shame — that nearly everyone would feel if they were in your shoes.

How I experience shame and guilt

SENSATIONS

Your cheeks get red and start to burn, your hands and feet grow numb, your head gets heavy, and your heart starts racing.

THOUGHTS

Everyone puts me down, nobody likes me, I must be a bad person, I'm such a loser, I wish I could disappear from the face of the Earth.

ACTIONS

You try to prove that you are in the right, you apologize, or simply go silent. You drop your gaze to avoid looking people in the eyes, you try to get away from people as soon as possible.

GUILT

A strong and unpleasant emotion we experience no matter whether we are surrounded by other people or on our own. It is a heavy burden bearing down on your shoulders, like a huge rock, preventing you from strolling through life with ease.

SHAME

You feel this **when you are put down or criticized by others**. Being shamed in public causes embarrassment and vulnerability. In such moments, we feel like we are naked and totally exposed. Words that people say and actions they take feel like rocks being thrown at us that can cause real pain.

DISCOMFORT

It is the weakest of unpleasant emotions **that we experience in public**. It causes uneasiness and makes you want to drop out of sight. It's like a tiny stone that's stuck in your shoe — you can only get rid of it once you have a chance to step away from everyone.

SHAME AND GUILT — WHAT'S THE DIFFERENCE?

You experience SHAME when people find out something about us that you wanted **to keep secret**. You may be ashamed for calling someone a name if it was overheard by others. Yet you don't feel any guilt for saying that, as it wasn't your intention to offend anyone. Shame comes from the outside, through the **opinions** and **judgment of other people**.

GUILT emerges when you break common norms or your own rules of behavior, when you hurt someone and feel **responsible** for that. For example, when you've been unnecessarily rude to another person, intending to offend him or her by design. Or when you've missed a training session even though you promised yourself you wouldn't. Guilt comes from **within** by **looking at yourself and making your own judgment about what you have or haven't done**.

Wouldn't life be great without guilt or shame?

It actually wouldn't as these emotions play an important role:

1. They give you a better understanding of your behavior: was this a good or a bad thing to do? Will there be consequences?

2. They help you take an outside look at yourself and grow as a person.

3. They help you find your place in society, make friends, and learn to love.

4. They caution you against doing something wrong — once you have felt shame or guilt, you try to avoid any actions that would cause such feelings again.

I apologize

Tips to overcoming shame and guilt

TALK TO OTHER PEOPLE

REFLECT

Did you have the opportunity to act differently? If you could not have influenced your course of action, or if you had no choice, then you should have no reason to blame yourself for what you did.

If there was an opportunity to act differently, and you made the wrong choice, forgive yourself and promise that you'll choose a different course next time.

We recommend viewing shame and guilt as inner signals that direct you to where you need to go and what you need to change.

It's better to be guided by universal standards and values, like being kind, noble and generous, than to focus on the opinions of a select few. Opinions that people might have about you may be very far from the truth. You are not responsible for their expectations.

If you have offended someone, accept responsibility and apologize. This will relieve you of this unpleasant worry you've been hauling around and will help you mend relations with the person.

If you're ashamed of what you have done — and rightfully so — admit it. Try to say, "I'm ashamed," and let this feeling come to the fore. Very often the best way to overcome an unpleasant emotion is just to acknowledge its right to exist.

I Feel Downhearted

There are days when you're in the dumps, and all you want to do is cry. Your friends have left for the summer, and there is nothing but melancholy and longing in your soul. You're sad about your parents always arguing. And when you look at yourself in the mirror, you're on the brink of despair. Is there any value in being so downhearted?

Totally downhearted

SENSATIONS
Zero energy, headache, heaviness, and emptiness inside, tears, shaking lips, a faltering voice, lump in the throat, urge to cry.

THOUGHTS
What have I done to deserve this? My life makes no sense. This is the end of the world. No one cares whether I exist or not.

ACTIONS
You seek seclusion, you listen to sad music, you wish there was someone to share your grief with, you stay in bed all day, you cry a lot.

MELANCHOLY AND SADNESS
They emerge from your being tired, from hearing bad news, or when bad things happen. Or for no apparent reason. Just like a cold drizzle, these emotions can go on for minutes or hours, and the whole world will look gray and unfriendly.

LONGING
You feel this when you think about a loved one who is not around. Or when you recall something good that will not happen again. While thoughts and memories are circling in your head, longing will continue. It's like a fog that envelops you and numbs the intensity of all your other feelings.

SORROW
A strong, usually unpleasant and long-lasting feeling. It emerges in response to dramatic events that have occurred to you or the people you care about. It's like an ice-cold shower that drenches you and darkens your thoughts.

Why do we need grief and sorrow?

 These emotions are an important mechanism that allow you to adapt to unpleasant events. It enables you to survive significant loss and avoid devastating trauma.

 They send signals to other people showing them that you're in trouble and that you need help and care.

 They ward off the effects of instability and constant change, which will be unavoidable aspects of the world around you throughout your entire life.

 They enable you to save energy in a difficult situation. They allow you to take a break from activities that are trying to suck up energy you currently don't have.

 They teach you the true value of the people and relationships you hold dear.

Learn to move on

Accept this feeling, it is not a sign of weakness. Say to it, "You have the right to exist."

Realize that you're suffering from a loss. Yes, it's painful, but that's the only way forward. Let yourself cry. It's not shameful, but rather very helpful.

Show some self-compassion. Take care of yourself by doing something that you enjoy doing.

They say that misery breaks hearts. In fact, misery opens up a heart, stripping it of its armor. This is the time to take care of your loved ones or reach out to them if you need help.

And remember, everything will pass. Even the most unbearable grief will not last forever.

Misery circles
Raindrops cause circles of different sizes on the water. In a similar manner, different **events trigger different ways to experience misery.**

Some people go through all misery's various circles, but others go through just a few. When misery subsides, tranquility takes over, just like water becoming placid again.

shock

denial

anger

attempts to fix everything

despair

humbleness and acceptance

GRIEF
This feeling consumes people entirely and for a long time. It follows a tragedy, such as a serious medical condition, separation from a loved one, or someone's death. Misery is more like a flood in which you find yourself drowning.

DESPAIR
The most intense and overwhelming state of weakness. People are in despair when they face an unsurmountable obstacle or a matter of life and death. It resembles an endless cold ocean where you find yourself without a life vest.

Emotions of Disgust

A new friend has turned out to be a disappointment. Lunch in the school cafeteria almost made you vomit. Your stupid classmates deserve only contempt, and you realize you can't stand your nagging teachers. You're not very happy with yourself either... What do you do when pretty much everything brings you down?

How will you know when you've reached your limit?

SENSATIONS

HATRED	DISGUST, CONTEMPT
Strength and energy, racing pulse.	Nausea, an unpleasant taste in your mouth.

THOUGHTS

I can't stand this! You're driving me nuts! Drop dead!	Gross, this is disgusting! I deserve better than this.

ACTIONS

You avoid contact or cause harm.	You display arrogance and express ridicule.

Things to consider if you hate and despise someone

- Does this person really deserve these feelings? If he hasn't done anything reprehensible, there should be no reason to despise or hate him.

- If the person deserves your scorn, try instead to forgive him or her. This is better than cultivating the hate and contempt that wells up inside.

- Try not to avoid judging people altogether. It's natural for people to have weaknesses and make mistakes. By accepting the mistakes of others, you give people a chance to mend their ways.

DISAPPOINTMENT
This is what you feel when something or someone has failed to meet your hopes or expectations. You would like your new friend to be communicative and show an interest in something. He or she isn't up to the task and now you're disappointed.

It's somewhat similar to putting on wet shoes — it's unlikely to cause you great harm, but it's definitely very unpleasant at first.

CONTEMPT
This emotion emerges when you place yourself above something or someone. You feel you're superior to others, like a swan among ugly ducklings.

When you despise yourself, it's the other way around. This is when YOU feel like an ugly duckling.

OVERALL DISGUST
It emerges in response to something off-putting that you find repugnant and would rather avoid.

It's that feeling you would get if a frog were to leap from a branch onto your neck and slide down your shirt.

Is there any benefit from these emotions?

Sure there is, just like from all the others.

They signal that **something is wrong** and that something requires your attention and possibly action.

Disappointment demonstrates the expectations you have for others and yourself.

Disgust teaches you to avoid things that are unpleasant, harmful, or infectious.

Contempt helps you figure out what personality traits or actions are unacceptable to you.

Hatred fuels you with the force and energy required to protect you from an enemy.

What's detrimental about them?

They ruin your **self-esteem.**

They cause **suffering** to you and others.

They result in **conflicts** with people, society, and even yourself.

They may cause serious **mental health issues** and trigger ill-conceived actions.

If that's how you feel about yourself...

 Start with accepting your right to be who you are. A lily does not hate itself for not being a rose. Everyone matters, and everyone has value.

 Identify your strengths and focus on them.

 Behave in the manner the perfect version of you would, the version of you that you feel deserves respect.

 Write down your victories. Forgive yourself for failures.

 Be mindful of your appearance but don't forget that it will change as you mature. Allow this process to proceed naturally.

HATRED
A powerful feeling of dislike and condemnation for someone. When you hate someone, you want to do him or her harm or simply hope you never see him or her again. This is often accompanied by intense anger, contempt, and a desire for revenge.

It's akin to a devastating tornado.

Allow yourself and others to be unique, as long as this uniqueness does not cause harm to anyone. **Nobody has to be perfect.**

Even an ugly duckling may turn into a beautiful swan at some point. **Learn to forgive yourself and others,** as this is the best cure for hatred, contempt, and disgust.

I Feel Unsettled, Even Scared

Do you get up in the morning thinking that the world is unsafe? Are you afraid of big dogs, being called on to speak in front of the class, or that you won't get any likes? This list can go on forever. We all have our own set of fears and concerns. Let's find out what they really mean.

When you're scared

SENSATIONS

A racing heartbeat, heavy and shaky legs, a dry mouth, sweaty palms.

THOUGHTS

This is dangerous, I'm scared, something bad is about to happen, I need to get out of here.

ACTIONS

You get away from the source of your fear and anxiety and you seek help and support.

Why you need these feelings

These are your most ancient emotional experiences. Today, just like a hundred thousand years ago, they:

- Warn you of danger.
- Boost your adrenaline to fight, flee, or improve yourself.
- Let others know that we need their protection.
- Bring people together in the face of danger.

UNEASE
A sense of danger or a premonition of failure. It's like the soundtrack of a horror film in your head warning you to "be careful!"

FEAR
It emerges when you encounter something that seems dangerous. For example, the fear of being home alone or the fear of making a fool of yourself in public. Fear is more intense than unease. But it passes more quickly.

TERROR
The most intense fear that a human can experience. It's like a powerful bell that tolls inside of you, making you completely focused on the threat.

When do you NOT need fear and anxiety?

Most people today don't live among wild animals or face primal dangers. Today many of our fears no longer help, but rather stand in the way of a peaceful existence.

○ They prevent you from trying anything new.

○ They are irrational — you're afraid of what is not really a threat.

○ They become a part of your routine and start dominating you.

○ They stand in the way of independence and self-sufficiency.

Tips to overcoming fear and anxiety

 Breathe. Five or six deep breaths in and out, which can turn fear into action thanks to the additional oxygen you are breathing in.

 Admit and observe. Give this emotion a name, look it straight in the eye. Speak to it, "This is fear. I am afraid." Focus on where in your body you sense fear and how it manifests itself.

 Ask yourself, "Is it real? Is there any reasoning behind my fears? Is there really anything that threatens me or my life?" Don't come up with future failures or horrible events.

 Thank your brain for its vigilance: "Thank you, my reptilian brain! However, I'm in no danger at the moment, so kindly go back to sleep."

 If you're concerned about something that is definitely going to occur, plan out your actions and reactions and be prepared.

Pause, Fight or Flee Response

In a situation where you experience fear, you can choose your strategy. Change your strategies, combine them, and experiment with them. Let your fears be the object of your research, not a roadblock to success!

FLEE — GIVE UP AND RUN FROM WHAT SCARES YOU	**PAUSE — COLLECT YOURSELF BEFORE DOING ANYTHING**	**FIGHT — OVERCOME YOUR FEARS AND SCARY SITUATIONS**
✓ **WHAT YOU CAN DO**		
If there's a real danger, like the sound of a car rapidly approaching, people suddenly behaving aggressively, or kids from your neighborhood suggesting that you try something illegal.	When you do nothing, this too can help you avoid danger. If you're afraid of saying something offensive to a friend out of anger, avoid the urge to speak and keep silent.	When your fear actually poses no real threat, like getting introduced to someone you like. Or a real threat, when you must act to save your own life, like pulling yourself out from under rubble.
✗ **WHAT YOU ARE BETTER OFF AVOIDING**		
When you experience fear due to your having doubt in your own abilities, like when your homework is frighteningly complicated.	When doing nothing may be dangerous, like when somebody is about to assault you, or you've been called on to give an answer in class.	When the danger you confront exceeds your ability to defend yourself, like when you confront an aggressive animal.

Is My Shyness My Fortress?

Studies have shown that five out of ten teenagers regularly experience shyness. Almost every tenth person experiences this all the time. This is a natural, but very delicate feeling that can push you to avoid contact. Let's try to minimize its effect a bit.

Embarrassment feels much like shame and guilt. But these are two different feelings.

When you're embarrassed...

SENSATIONS

You have a lumpy throat, body shivers, flushed face, hyperventilation, rapid heartbeat, sweaty palms.

THOUGHTS

I wish I could drop off the face of the earth. No one is going to like me. They'll just diss me. I don't deserve their attention.

ACTIONS

You hide your eyes, keep silent or speak quietly. You try to avoid interaction with people, and shy away from new people.

SHAME AND GUILT
Both in public and while on your own.

EMBARRASSMENT
Only while in public.

But frequent and intense embarrassment may bring you to feel shame for your shyness and make you blame yourself for your reserved behavior.

Feeling timid, embarrassed, bashful, or shy?

These all are **different names of the same feeling**, one that causes you to feel tense when you communicate with people and leaves you feeling lost and very uncomfortable. For a shy person, communication with others feels a lot like defending a fortress under attack.

SLIGHTLY TIMID
It's like a glass door that separates you from people. You can open it on your own, you just need to make a little effort and establish contact, maybe by simply smiling at somebody in return, or extending your hand.

FAIRLY TIMID
It's similar to a high fence that cordons you off from people. In order to cross that fence, you need to find a hole in it: finding the right word to start a conversation, making eye contact, or being the first to speak.

FULL-ON TOO SCARED TO INTERACT
It's like an unassailable castle where you are the lone prisoner. You can break out, but this will require an enormous amount of energy and bravery. Sometimes this level of timidity plagues your life so bad that you are angry both at yourself and the world. And then the furious dragon finally bursts out of its fortress...

What can you gain from being embarrassed?

What harm can come from being embarrassed?

LIGHT EMBARRASSMENT:
- Prevents you from being too open with strangers.
- Allows you to be cautious in new situations.

INTENSE EMBARRASSMENT:
- Gets in your way when you want to communicate with new people.
- Rachets up your anxiety.
- Prevents you from speaking out and standing up for your rights.
- Deprives others of the ability to understand your thoughts.
- Stops you from asking others for help.

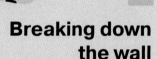

Breaking down the wall

Trying to overcome a permanent state of embarrassment is like breaking down your inner fortress stone by stone.

 Accept that embarrassment is a **normal reaction** to an unfamiliar situation. You're not the only one who experiences this feeling.

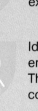 Identify the situations and people that make you feel embarrassed: these are your **embarrassment zones**. Then figure which situations and people boost your confidence: these are your **confidence zones**.

 Turn your embarrassment zones into confidence zones step by step: overcome embarrassment and celebrate the little victories.

 When you talk to new people, focus more **on them** rather than on yourself. They too might feel awkward and need your help.

Communication is a two-way street. Success depends on both sides pulling their weight. You don't have to take on full responsibility for the conversation.

Observe and emulate. When you find yourself in comfortable situations, emulate successful moves, phrases, and gestures of those whom you consider masters of communication.

Booorring!

School is a total bore. At home you're powerless to force yourself to do your homework or your chores. Even getting outside is no longer exciting. You browse through your socials aimlessly, killing time like it's endless. Sounds like you are dealing with some serious boredom.

When you're bored stiff

SENSATIONS

You're empty, time passes slowly, you see futility in everything, and just feel like napping all the time.

THOUGHTS

You feel no excitement, you wish the day would hurry up and end, you desperately need something to do.

ACTIONS

You're always horizontal, you sleep a lot, you browse through socials to no end, and when you do something, you do it mechanically.

BOREDOM AS A LIMITING FACTOR

It rears its head when you must do something that you find dull and senseless. This kind of boredom is like a handbrake that slows down your energy and activity level, stalling whatever progress you are making and turning your activities into routine.

IT'S MOSTLY A BAD THING BECAUSE:

- you can't follow through on important, but unexciting things you need to get done
- you feel tired and exhausted
- you blame yourself for wasted time or unfinished business

PRODUCTIVE BOREDOM

It emerges when you want to do something but are unable to find anything exciting. It feels like an unexpected gap in your list of activities you now want to fill.

IT'S MOSTLY A GOOT THING BECAUSE:

- you get an opportunity to relax
- you may get the urge to try something new and creative
- you brainstorm, experiment, and become innovative

Why am I bored?

As a rule, **boredom is a feeling people experience when they're by themselves**. When you are accustomed to doing things with others, you may find yourself at a loss when you're all by alone.

What's more, people **have become used to always being occupied**, listening to or watching something. Our lives are pretty much devoid of moments of silence. We fear them and rush to fill in these holes.

At the same time, it is **solitude and silence** that provide you with the time and space you need for yourself, your own ideas, thoughts, and inventions.

Making good use of boredom

 Accept boredom: it's the downtime you need for your personal development!

 Spend some time in silence while doing nothing. Notice what you feel, what thoughts come to mind.

 Write down your ideas, thoughts, and feelings.

 If your boredom does not give way to creative ideas, try something new. Maybe it's time to start dancing, drawing, making collages? Or is there some hobby you've always been putting off that is still waiting for you?

Using your limitations to become more productive

○ Try to find some meaning in everything you do. Ask yourself and others, "Why does this need to be done?" If you acknowledge that there is meaning in your activity, desire and excitement will follow.

○ Devise new ways of doing things that bore you. Try brushing your teeth with your left hand. Alternate your routine to include exciting and unexciting things.

○ If it's super dull, try doing it for time. Boring tasks may become more interesting to complete if you set yourself a time limit.

○ Watch your peers and adults: that's how you can pick up new ideas on things you can do.

Wow!
What a Surprise!

Curiosity drives us forward when we study, work, or fall in love. It pushes us towards discoveries and accomplishments. Curiosity is always followed by delight and surprise, which make us feel happiness. Here's the key to a life full of joy!

When you're intrigued and surprised

SENSATIONS

Your pulse decreases, you have bated breath, you experience shivers all over your body.

THOUGHTS

What is going on? Why is this happening? I need to know! Wow! Now we're talkin'!

ACTIONS

You're trying new things, you're overwhelmed with surprise, you're jumping for joy.

CURIOSITY AND EXCITEMENT

These feelings are your inner lens through which you look at the world, study it in details, and uncover its secrets. Only intense and unpleasant emotions can temporarily cloud your lens.

SURPRISE

A fleeting feeling that seems like a momentary gust of wind. It emerges immediately in response to something unexpected and totally new. You may be surprised with a birthday present or the results of your test.

JOY

A combination of surprise and intense elation, a feeling of joy can overtake you suddenly when you come face to face with something magnificent and exciting. Your insides experience fireworks that make you want to jump, and your positive emotions illuminate you like bright lights.

Why do I need these feelings?

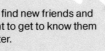
You dive headfirst into an exciting activity, oblivious to any fatigue.

You realize what occupation and hobbies you want to choose in life.

You want to learn new things and self-develop all the time.

You find new friends and want to get to know them better.

You deal with fear, concerns, boredom, laziness, and other unpleasant emotions more easily.

You feel a huge inflow of energy and happiness.

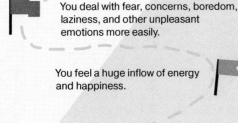

Curiosity, surprise, and joy serve as **sources of energy for your batteries**. Collect and commit such moments to memory by writing them down in a diary or in drawings. This is your **positive energy** bank, which you can always tap into during difficult moments.

When nobody shares my interests

Your curiosity and excitement may not necessarily be supported by others. If your interest is not dangerous for yourself or people around you, and if it also gives you a lot of joy, don't give up on your idea!

People often fail to understand why you waste time on an activity that they consider boring. Who cares what they think?

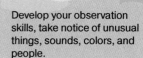

Tips to preserving your inquisitiveness and the ability to be surprised

Try to remember that the world is full of secrets. It will have enough to surprise you with until the end of your days (provided that you take off your know-it-all spectacles).

Don't be afraid to pursue your interests, even if they're unpopular and not shared by anyone.

Try all kinds of activities — experiment.

Develop your observation skills, take notice of unusual things, sounds, colors, and people.

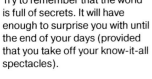

Look for unusual things in your daily routine. There are new things to be discovered even in the classroom.

Focus on sensations that you feel during moments when you are pleasantly surprised, curious, and experiencing joy.

Surprise others with your creativity and kindness. Share your joy and curiosity, as these feelings are 'contagious'.

I'm So Offended!

Somebody has unfriended you on your socials. A teacher gave you a bad grade on your homework. A friend forgot to say happy birthday. On the surface, it's not a big deal, yet you can feel the bitterness welling up inside. It's saying to you, "You've been treated unfairly. You're the victim. They're to blame." Do you always need to listen to it?

How do you know when someone has offended you?

SENSATIONS

Bad mood, tears welling up in your eyes, a lump in your throat.

THOUGHTS

It's not my fault I feel this way. This is not fair. I'm not the one who needs to apologize.

ACTIONS

You ghost your offenders, you demand an apology, you become contemptuous, or you simply start crying.

Bitterness comes from the realization that **somebody has intentionally treated you poorly or unfairly**. This is one of the most persistent of feelings. People can remain bitter for many years in hopes that an apology will set them free. However, **apologies don't help — only forgiveness can**! And you can forgive your offender without waiting for an apology.

MALICIOUS BITTERNESS

It's bitterness working in cohorts with spite and hatred. Your inner dragon's flaming breath will dry your tears and boost your energy and self-confidence. You no longer feel like the victim. You are now seeking revenge.

ARROGANT BITTERNESS

You believe that your offender only deserves your contempt. You now look down on him, showing him that you want nothing to do with him. Contempt may gradually turn into hatred. You're no longer simply offended, but rather you begin to hate that person.

SORROWFUL BITTERNESS

You become sad and no longer want to communicate. You want to stay on your own and think everything over. This kind of bitterness does not cause any harm. But if it lingers on, it can drench you with an ice-cold shower of sorrow.

ENVIOUS BITTERNESS

This emerges when you start comparing yourself to others and the result is not in your favor. You figure out that the world is unfair to you. You start feeling envious and bitter towards people.

Tips for overcoming bitterness

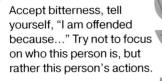

Accept bitterness, tell yourself, "I am offended because…" Try not to focus on who this person is, but rather this person's actions.

Do not fuel your bitterness by thinking that other people are bad, or that the world is unfair.

Ask yourself, "Has this person wronged me on purpose, by mistake, or accidentally?" Sometimes people's actions are like bad weather — it's unexpected and unpleasant, but not malicious.

What is making us upset?

Have you ever been upset by bad weather? Or by a cat that doesn't want to play with you? It's highly unlikely. The thing is that people don't believe that the weather is out to ruin their day, or that pets no longer love them. You only get upset about the actions of **other people** — those whom we know, whom we care about, and who we expect to behave in some specific manner. When their actions deviate from how you would like them to behave, we find this offensive.

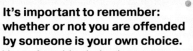

It's important to remember: whether or not you are offended by someone is your own choice. Very often this choice is not even based on reality. It's very seldom that somebody wants to offend us on purpose. Yet, this is one of the most common negative feelings.

Carrying a grudge is dangerous. It destroys you from within and causes more harm to you than to your offender. The resulting bitterness is a complex feeling that rarely emerges in isolation, but rather together with other negative emotions.

You can't always judge a person by his or her actions

If you speak to a person about being hurt by his or her actions, the offender will have a much better idea about what can or cannot be done to preserve good relations. If you speak about being hurt by a person (not actions), the offender will defend him or herself and your relations will suffer.

Character vs behavior

Try to determine whether you have been offended by a person, or the person's actions. If you identify the action that has caused your bitterness correctly, you will not be offended for long, as such emotions are survivable and can be mended quickly. It will also be easier to talk about them: "What you said about me really offended me" is not the same as "You hate me, you're a bad person."

Recall instances when you have hurt people, too — not because you wanted to, but mostly due to some misunderstanding.

Share your feelings with your offender, give him or her a chance to understand what went wrong and make amends. But don't demand an apology, allow the person to make this choice on his or her own.

Forgive the person in your mind, even if he or she hasn't apologized, and accept the person's imperfection. To forgive is the best way to drop the burden of carrying bitterness.

What Is Happiness?

We all dream of being happy. But we all have to choose our own way of getting there. Let's chart your road to sustainable happiness.

Does your happiness come from the outside or inside?

Imagine that your most sacred wish has come true. For instance, you just received a brand-new smartphone. How long will you be on cloud nine? Is it going to be a day, two days, or a week?

This euphoria will pass soon, and you'll find yourself dreaming about something else. Why does this happen? It's because we're speaking about an **external source** of happiness, which simply is not sustainable.

Internal sources

True happiness grows from within. It's as if it's illuminating everything inside and outside of you, filling your body with strength and easiness. Happiness fuels your energy, allowing you to overcome difficult obstacles and implement the most daring plans.

Your unique goal or purpose

If you succeed in finding an activity that combines your interests and strengths, and that will create new goals for you that you will enjoy reaching, you will have made a huge investment in your sustainable happiness.

Relationships

Being in a strong relationship is a truly reliable sources of happiness. A major Harvard study, which has been in progress for more than 80 years, has shown that there's nothing more important than the quality of your relations and regular contact with others. No education, money, or social status are enough to compensate for the absence of a close relationship.

Consciousness and living in the moment

Learn to live and value every minute as if is your last. Tranquility, silence, and contemplation allow you to stay in touch with yourself and the world.

Taking care of other people

In addition, you have the ability to help people, animals, plants, and the planet selflessly. Altruism, compassion, and caring for others create even more benefits for the giver than the receiver.

We feel joy and brief happiness thanks to specific things or occurrences. They differ from one person to the next: it may be some brand of clothing, a good grade on a test, or a long-awaited trip.

External sources

Find that perfect place for feeling joy from external sources (don't think that happiness depends only on them) and learn how to immerse yourself fully into this state.

Do you remember how high your hopes were that you would get an A for the year in Literature? When you finally got that A, the joy only lasted a day or two. Similarly, a successful post quickly loses its relevance, a new smartphone model is soon followed by an even cooler one... You get the point.

Does it mean that the joy you get from specific events or material things is not real? No, it most certainly is. External sources of joy are indeed important. This type of short-term happiness is also capable of giving you energy and supporting you in difficult periods.

Tips to savoring quick moments of happiness

Don't get too used to them

Our ability to adapt quickly results in our quickly passing through moments of happiness as we easily take them for granted.

- Stop and seize your joy.
- Feel gratitude for its existence.
- Surprise yourself and others more often so that joy is not provided according to some schedule.

Take it all in!

- Share your joy with others.
- Seize it so that you can later tap into your 'happiness bank' (maintain a happiness log, take photos, or draw pictures).
- Be proud, congratulate yourself, and celebrate.

If you become happy, will all your problems suddenly disappear?

No, they won't. You will continue to be confronted by complex situations, and unpleasant feelings will visit you just like before — there are no exceptions for anyone. The difference is, your problems will not seem so impossible to resolve and won't drive you to depression or weigh you down. Why? Because your inner sources of happiness are always with you!

Practicing gratitude

There is a very easy way at your disposal right now for doing this. The more you focus on what you have and what you're good at, and feel grateful for that, the more intense your inner joy is.

Practicing gratitude

- Say thank you to the people around you who help and take care of you.
- Keep a diary of gratitude: write down five things for which you are grateful at the end of each day.
- Thank yourself more often: for being optimistic, for getting things done, for gaining new knowledge. For everything you can be proud of.

Curiosity and optimism

These are personal traits that you can develop. Many studies mention these human qualities as key to achieving sustainable happiness.

Where Does Love Come From?

Is it from your family? From nature, friends, or music? Or the kind heart of the person whom you've been looking forward to meeting? Here is a secret: love lives within you! The only thing you need in order to feel it more often is to look inward, maintain a connection with it, and share it with the world!

Loving yourself

Parents, friends, and family support us with their love from day one. As we grow up, we keep on believing that love comes from the outside, that it must be continually sourced from someone else.

What is this source of love? **It's within you!** Right now, you can get as much love as you need. Let's see if we can find some.

RECIPE FOR LOVE

A + A

Accepting the unconditional value of life, both yours and that of another person.

Accepting yourself and others fully (including their entire set of individualities, capabilities, and limitations).

Sometimes it may seem that you don't get enough love. It's times like these when people begin blaming themselves and believing that something is wrong with them. They try to solve the mystery of why they have little or no love in their lives. They do this in several ways.

COMPETITION

PERFECTIONISM

DENIAL

If I'm better than others, then I deserve love. It's a tried-and-true way to lose contact with the world and the most important thing in it, which is being in a true relationship. The satisfaction you may get from feeling superior to others is only fleeting. Such victories only help build a wall of vanity between you and the world, while your defeats contribute equally to the wall of resentment and self-deprecation you've built. Try to cooperate, not compete, and you will quickly see the difference.

I must be perfect to get love. This is a road that leads to continuous disappointment. Your focus on perfecting yourself endlessly results in your paying attention only to what requires reworking. By denying the existence of what you don't like in yourself, you dismiss yourself as a person. Treating yourself this way is biased and not constructive.

I don't need anybody. This is the attitude of a resentful child, which ultimately drives people to reclusion and profound misery. Enjoy your feelings of love and affection, do not suppress them!

A+R

Accepting your right to personal liberty and freedom of expression.

Respecting yourself and other people unconditionally without any reservations.

Share love. The mathematics of love is peculiar: the more you give, the more you get. Take care of people, animals, and nature. You will soon realize that your source of love has no bounds.

Surround yourself with supportive people. Your friends, acquaintances, and family love you and can put together an entire list of your merits. They can even love you for no special reason. You should learn from them!

Treat yourself like the valuable person you are. Award yourself with small prizes, take care of your body, treat yourself to a tasty snack. Do something that you really love, while not evaluating how good you are at it, or trying to make it perfect.

Don't abandon yourself in tough times. If you find yourself in a difficult situation, or if you've fallen ill, take note and acknowledge that you're suffering. Show compassion and sympathy to yourself.

Practice self-acceptance. On a daily basis, note three things in yourself that make you proud and satisfied. Gradually add your weaknesses one by one, treating them with humor and being ready to accept them.

Forgive yourself for everything that has caused you pain, disappointment, or bitterness. Tell yourself, "I forgive myself for this mistake, I am only learning to live, I will try to do better next time." Criticizing and chastising oneself has never helped anyone become better. This only makes people more insecure.

Fears related to self-acceptance:

If I accept and love myself, then there's no motivation for me to develop myself

Negative motivation is a weak tool and is effective for only a short while. If you develop the habit of getting rid of all your shortcomings, merits will simply fall out of sight. Loving oneself serves as **positive motivation for development**: the person you love deserves better.

If I love and accept myself, am I being egoistic?

Egoism means putting your interests above another person's interests. Loving oneself offers an example of a proper relationship: **valuing and accepting the other person unconditionally**. Meanwhile, loving somebody else unconditionally is very difficult if you haven't tried it on yourself and figured out how it works.

Too Many Emotions All at Once

A particular event may trigger an entire slew of feelings, where one is hiding behind another, and you have no idea how to sort them out. Have you ever been confused like that and were somewhat slow to react?

When your emotions start to add up

Emotions and feelings may begin to accumulate and form emotional blocks:

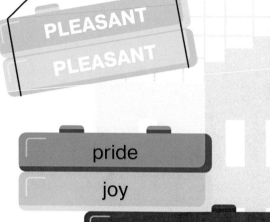

PLEASANT
PLEASANT

pride
joy
love
excitement
surprise
happiness

UNPLEASANT
PLEASANT

guilt
pride
surprise
terror

interest
disgust

Such blocks may bring together two, three, or even more emotions and/or feelings. They are like the pieces of a building set with which we try to build our unique inner world.

UNPLEASANT
UNPLEASANT

resentment
anger
shame
guilt
sadness
fear
disgust

Even though you may feel all of these emotions simultaneously, **you can choose to focus on the dominant emotion** at any given moment.

Why would you allow the little things (the catering was not great, and very few people enjoyed the food) to spoil the big picture (it was a great party)?

PLEASANT TO UNPLEASANT

A teacher has given you an A and spoke highly of your preparedness. You feel pride, joy, and gratitude, which is an entire block of pleasant emotions.

Gratitutde toward your teacher

joy for yourself — pride in yourself

Meanwhile, the teacher gives a B- to your friend who knows the answers just as well as you do. You may develop guilt and disappointment. Now your block is more complex due to the addition of unpleasant emotions.

disappointment in your teacher — guilt for your friend

joy for yourself — pride in yourself

Now imagine that the teacher has given an A+ to another classmate and spoke even more highly of him than you! You may develop envy and anger at your classmate and resentment against your teacher. Some feelings get replaced with others just like pieces of a building set.

envy of your classmate

anger at your classmate

disappointment in your teacher

resentment against your teacher

Here's how several intense unpleasant emotions can overrun pleasant ones.

UNPLEASANT TO PLEASANT

It can work the other way around as well. Unpleasant emotions and feelings are the first to emerge, and pleasant ones will soon follow. Your parents have told you that you're going to summer camp. You don't want to go, because you want to spend the summer here with your friends. You're concerned that you won't be able to find a common language with your campmates. You're concerned that it may be boring there. You feel bitterness and anger at your parents because they wouldn't listen to you.

anger at your parents

resentment at your parents

anticipation of upcoming boredom

anxiety about getting to know new people

sadness about separation from friends

However, you get to know from your socials that a few students from your school whom you like are going to the same camp. You are excited and happy. Finally, you will get a chance to know them and have fun together.

gratitude to your parents for the opportunity to go to camp

joy about meeting new acquaintances

interest in your classmates

Here's how pleasant feelings can eclipse unpleasant ones.

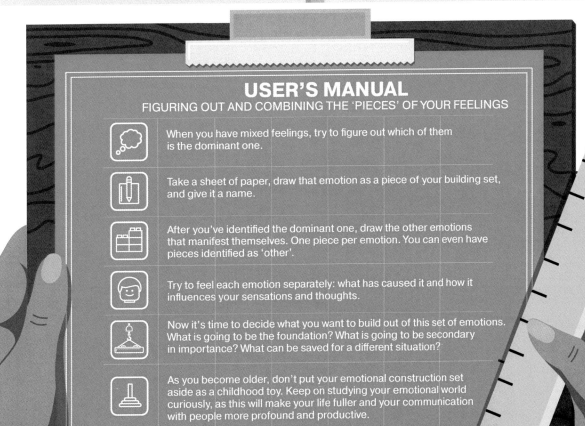

USER'S MANUAL
FIGURING OUT AND COMBINING THE 'PIECES' OF YOUR FEELINGS

When you have mixed feelings, try to figure out which of them is the dominant one.

Take a sheet of paper, draw that emotion as a piece of your building set, and give it a name.

After you've identified the dominant one, draw the other emotions that manifest themselves. One piece per emotion. You can even have pieces identified as 'other'.

Try to feel each emotion separately: what has caused it and how it influences your sensations and thoughts.

Now it's time to decide what you want to build out of this set of emotions. What is going to be the foundation? What is going to be secondary in importance? What can be saved for a different situation?

As you become older, don't put your emotional construction set aside as a childhood toy. Keep on studying your emotional world curiously, as this will make your life fuller and your communication with people more profound and productive.

What's Next?

Things to keep in mind

- What feeling do you regard as the most intense?
- What would you like to feel more often? How can you help that?
- Is there an unpleasant feeling that you have been living with for a long time? How can you express it?
- Do you feel love for yourself? How is it manifested?

Listening quest: experience feelings through music

Emotions are the music of the soul. Composers create music primarily to address feelings. Music helps you identify, experience, and let go of feelings. Sometimes you can travel back to a feeling with just the right music.

We have put together a list of 12 musical pieces, each expressing a particular feeling. Listen to them and try to guess which feeling each piece expresses.

Giuseppe Verdi.
Dies Irae. Performed by Teodor Currentzis
 1

2
Pyotr Ilyich Tchaikovsky.
Trepak (Russian Dance) from **The Nutcracker.**
Performed by the State Academic Bolshoi Theatre
Orchestra

Johannes Brahms.
Symphony No. 3, Third Movement. Performed by
the University of Music Franz Liszt Weimar Orchestra
 3

4
Alessandro Marcello.
**Oboe Concerto for oboe and strings. Adagio
in D minor.** Performed by the Royal Philharmonic
Orchestra

Gustav Holst.
Uranus, the Magician. Performed by the BBC
Philharmonic Orchestra
 5

6
Alfred Schnittke.
Agony: Waltz. Performed by the USSR
Cinematography Symphony Orchestra

Pyotr Ilyich Tchaikovsky.
Arabian Dance from **The Nutcracker.** Performed by
the State Academic Bolshoi Theatre Orchestra
7

8
Sergei Rachmaninov.
Prelude in C-sharp minor. Performed by Nikolai
Lugansky

Joseph Haydn.
Piano Sonata in D Major, Hob. XVI/37. Performed
by Jean-Efflam Bavouzet
9

10
Pyotr Ilyich Tchaikovsky.
The Witch (Baba Yaga). Performed by Mikhail
Pletnev

Frederic Chopin.
Nocturne in D-flat major, Op. 27, No. 2.
Performed by Yulianna Avdeeva
11

12
Ludwig van Beethoven.
Symphony No. 5.
Performed by the Berlin Philharmonic

○ Embarrassment

○ Love

○ Shame

○ Boredom

○ Disgust and hatred

○ Fear

○ Anger

○ Sadness

○ Complex emotions

○ Bitterness

○ Joy and happiness

○ Surprise and curiosity

CHAPTER 4
Getting Along With Your Feelings

Can You Hide From Your Feelings

Sometimes you want to feel nothing at all or switch off emotions that you don't like. Is it possible? Let's think of common ways people try to get rid of unpleasant feelings. Are they helpful?

1 Playing hide-and-seek with your emotions

...Ready or not, here I come!

Have you ever been ashamed for feeling a certain emotion, like anger? Have you ever been run down by emotions that are just too intense? Have your emotions ever been too complex or entangled? In such cases, people often choose to play hide-and-seek with their feelings, meaning they pretend that they don't feel anything.
It's like you're trying to plug your ears and pretend that you don't hear the voice that is warning you of danger.
But emotions will not go away. They too will play hide-and-seek, meaning they'll hide behind other feelings and actions and will continue consuming your attention and energy.

Am I hiding good enough?

FEAR
hides behind anger or laziness.

ENVY
hides behind indignation or criticism.

BITTERNESS
hides behind irritation or indifference.

2 Swat the feeling away like a fly or 'Feelings are for the weak'

Many people believe that only the weak display their feelings, while tough people always keep everything under control. This is a dangerous misconception!

I couldn't care less

First, this feeling will not go away. It will instead stay within you and find an even louder way to remind you of itself.

Second, you may miss an important signal that the emotion is trying to send you.

Third, this method requires enormous energy and willpower, usurping them from other problem areas that also need attention.

Last, but not least, people who are strong in spirit are not afraid to accept their human nature and can embrace their emotions.

3 Rip and tear — set your emotions free!

This is yet another dangerous way of dealing with feelings that has become popular in recent decades. If you're angry, scream; if somebody hits you, hit him or her back. Let your dragon fly free!

Do you think this method is constructive? What are the consequences?

A wild outburst of unpleasant emotions scares and hurts those around you and only multiplies negative energy. When people are driven by emotions, they often do things that they will later regret.

This is my turf!

Why is it dangerous to set free reckless emotions?

WHEN YOU'RE FURIOUS:
- You lose contact with reality.
- You may hurt yourself or others.
- You may break or destroy something valuable, including friendships and love.

WHEN YOU'RE ANGRY:
- It's difficult for people to understand you, because your emotions make your thoughts and words confusing.
- You accuse people of being something they are not.
- You're being narrow-minded, you're seeing the world through a tiny lens.

WHEN YOU'RE SCARED:
- You want to run away, without even trying to find out if there's really any danger.
- Small things seem like insurmountable issues.
- You refuse to try, which leaves you with no chance to overcome fear.

WHEN YOU'RE UPSET:
- You give up and abandon the thing you've started.
- You stop believing in yourself and others.

Why is it bad to try to suppress unpleasant emotions?

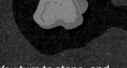

You turn to stone, and you stop feeling pleasant emotions too.

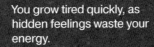

You grow tired quickly, as hidden feelings waste your energy.

You develop medical conditions that may stay with you for a long time.

You stop understanding yourself and others. Your relations begin to fall apart.

Just Stop and Observe? Really?

We have concluded that simply controlling your emotions is not the best way to make peace with them. Then what exactly are you supposed to do? Learn to take a break and observe yourself. But how?

As Mom used to say, "Look at yourself through other people's eyes."

Have you noticed that you have started using filler words? "Well," "like," "kinda…" — such words are in abundance these days. You probably realize that it's actually very easy to get rid of them: just start noting them in your speech. You can even count them if you want to amplify the effect. Give it a try.

It turns out that by detaching yourself from the subject of your observations and keeping it at arm's length, you gain much strength from this and can even master a superpower. This is not only applicable with words, but it's also applicable to our emotions.

1 STOP AND TAKE A BREAK

Taking a break means saying and doing nothing when you're overtaken by emotions. This break will help you see clearly what's going on. The brain will not get distracted by additional signals, and you will regain your grasp of reality.

Are you experiencing a strong emotion and itching to react immediately?

- Stop.
- Take a short break.
- Breathe.
- Observe yourself.

2 BREATHE

BREATHE IN
Put one hand on your stomach and the other one on your chest to sense how you're breathing. Close your eyes and take a deep breath through your nose as you count to three or four.

PAUSE
Hold your breath as you count to three or four.

BREATHE OUT
Breathe out slowly after you count to three or four, you can do it through your mouth. Imagine that you are releasing your emotions with the exhaled air.

PAUSE
If a thought or a new surge of emotions surfaces, don't get mad at yourself. Just focus once again on the sensations in your body and continue breathing.

Sometimes one 'breathe in — pause — breathe out' cycle is enough to recover your senses. When emotions are intense, several attempts may be required.

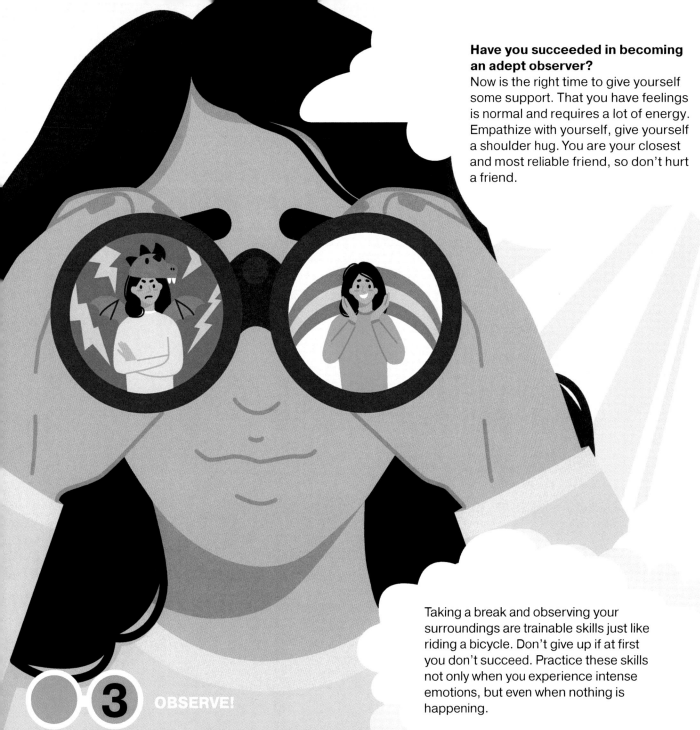

Have you succeeded in becoming an adept observer?
Now is the right time to give yourself some support. That you have feelings is normal and requires a lot of energy. Empathize with yourself, give yourself a shoulder hug. You are your closest and most reliable friend, so don't hurt a friend.

Taking a break and observing your surroundings are trainable skills just like riding a bicycle. Don't give up if at first you don't succeed. Practice these skills not only when you experience intense emotions, but even when nothing is happening.

③ OBSERVE!

It's time to describe what's going on. Avoid judgment, just name specific objects and occurrences.

Wrong:
The teacher is too judgmental, he obviously hates me.

Right:
The teacher has simply asked me a question.

Ask yourself:

- What am I feeling? What is this feeling called? Let it exist.

- Where do I feel it in my body?

- What beliefs or attitudes have triggered this feeling in me?

Dealing with Emotions: Accept and Let Go*

Stopping and observing a feeling at arm's length is a productive way of coping with a sudden surge of emotions. An emotion, just like physical pain arrives on the scene to tell people something important. If people pretend that they're not home, then they never get to hear this important message.

How do you truly hear what your visiting emotion is telling you?

1 OPEN THE DOOR AND SAY HELLO

Take a break. Listen to your body, sense the emotion it is conveying. Open your mind to that emotion: "I feel…" Call it by the name and say hello, make it clear that it is welcome.

Well, hello there, fear!

Greetings, anger! So that's what you look like!

Nice to meet you, sadness.

2 LET IT IN

Let the emotion manifest itself within you for all it's worth. Experience how it expresses itself in your body, take notice of the thoughts that accompany it. Don't let these thoughts whisk you away. Watch from the outside, just like a host watches his guest.

At this stage, you may become ashamed of the emotion, or you may have the desire to send it away or express it. There's nothing to be ashamed of, it's only visiting. It needs your attention and assistance.

* Based on RAIN practice by meditation teacher Michele McDonald

Obviously you will continue to feel your visitor's presence for a while after the visit. But its impact will no longer be heavy or intense. And it will soon give way to something more relevant.

The most important thing is that the visitor will not have to nag you to be heard. It will come back, but for a new reason and with a new message.

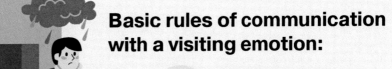

Basic rules of communication with a visiting emotion:

Don't denounce, judge, or criticize your visitor. It needs help!

Treat any emotion with love and kindness.

You are the master of your house.

Be an observer.

5 LET IT GO IN PEACE AND WITH GRATITUDE

Show the visitor to the door and give it a hug goodbye.

> Thank you, anger! I understand what you wanted to tell me. I hear you. Thank you for the information. You may go now.

> Thank you, my reptile brain! I know that you wanted to warn me of danger. There is nothing to be afraid of at the moment. You may take a rest.

4 GIVE IT SOME TEA AND TAKE GOOD CARE

Remember that your visitor is that part of you that is experiencing emotion. It needs care and love, not blame and criticism. The visitor might like drinking a cup of tea or listening to some music.

You can support yourself physically by putting your hand on the part of your body that most keenly feels the emotion, or you can hug your own shoulders.

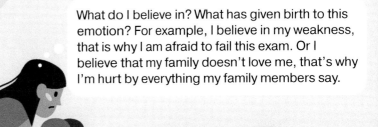

3 HEAR IT OUT

You don't need to do anything, just listen to your visitor. This may be a warning of danger, a cry for help from your self-esteem, or pain from losing something important.

> What do you want to tell me?

What do I believe in? What has given birth to this emotion? For example, I believe in my weakness, that is why I am afraid to fail this exam. Or I believe that my family doesn't love me, that's why I'm hurt by everything my family members say.

Who's There in Your Head: A Critic or Supporter?

Feelings and thoughts are parts of the same mechanism within you. They are strongly connected with one another, just like two gear-wheels. A feeling can generate literally thousands of thoughts. Pleasant feelings generate pleasant thoughts, and vice versa. But what are you supposed to do if your thoughts are fueled by unpleasant emotions? How do you break this connection?

Mindset, or Two lenses

The same occurrences may launch a circulation of pleasant or unpleasant thoughts and feelings. It all depends on the lens that you use when observing yourself and the world.

Gray lens
If you believe that everything's a mess, that you are good for nothing, or that nothing good is ever going to occur, then negative thoughts will bring about unpleasant feelings, and vice versa.

Orange lens
If you are confident about your future, if you accept yourself, and love life, then positive thoughts will trigger pleasant feelings, which, in turn, will contribute to your positive thinking.

You lack self-confidence and are wary of everything around you

You are secure and open to people and the world

THOUGHTS	FEELINGS
I'm never lucky	Disappointment
My super old jacket totally sucks	Confusion
I will stick out like a sore thumb	Shame
I look like the worst in any crowd	Envy
My parents don't buy me anything, while my sister gets everything	Jealousy
They don't let me do anything	Anger
I don't want to help them! Leave me alone!	

Great, now I've got a stain on my jacket...

THOUGHTS	FEELINGS
I will be more cautious next time	Concentration
Dry-cleaning might help	Tranquility
Or it'll be a reason to update my wardrobe	Joy
I can go shopping with my friend	Anticipation
It's great that I have such a friend	Excitement
It's time to get my closet in order and get rid of the things I don't need	

Tips to changing your lens

Have you noticed how your thought-emotion cycle keeps going round and round again? Look at it from the outside and ask yourself, "What lens am I using?"

You're a good-for-nothing!

A slow-poke!

goofball!

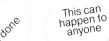

Mean critic

Your critic notices the smallest mistakes or drawbacks and compares you to others. The critic is always dissatisfied with what you do and how you do it. The things you hear from your critic make you sad, your self-esteem suffers, and you just want to give up everything and run away.

Listen to yourself: what is your inner voice telling you? Is it disparaging or supportive? The thing that is tearing you apart is your inner **Detractor**. The voice that is cheering you on is your **Supporter**. If you don't do anything about it, you will always hear just one of them, and most likely it will be your detractor. But if you become friends with yourself, both voices will be your helpers for life.

Well done

This can happen to anyone

Way to go!

Kind supporter

On the contrary, your supporter will cheer you up in difficult situations. The supporter is always at your side, standing up for you, helping you to pull yourself together, and making sure that you believe in yourself.

What can you do about your critic?

Think whose voice you hear in your head when you're mad at yourself. Is this what your strict teacher used to say? Or was it somebody in your family? A critic's voice usually sounds to you like the voice of someone who matters.

 Is your inner critic competent in the things he's tearing you apart over? Maybe asking an expert for advice or an unbiased assessment would do?

 Is the critic calling you names or being rude? You are fully entitled to switch off his microphone. Non-constructive remarks have no value.

 If you want to separate yourself from your critic's voice, you can assume the role or an observer on a more frequent basis. Keep on asking yourself, "What is it that I believe in that caused this thought? What emotions are triggered by this thought? Do I want to think and feel this way?"

How can you amplify the supporter's voice?

The supporter talks to you through the voices of those who love you. These are your friends and family. If you don't get enough support and approval in tough situations, just imagine what your loved ones would tell you. And remember, you are your **kindest and most reliable friend, the one who will never abandon you**.

Emotion Lab: What Else Affects Me?

Just yesterday you were happy spending time with friends, but today you want to get home as soon as possible.
One day you won't even notice that you got a bad grade, while the next day it will feel like it's the end of the world. The situations seem to be the same, but your reactions are totally different. What is the reason?

What do feelings consist of?

Imagine that there's a complex laboratory working inside you day and night, continually mixing numerous ingredients in test tubes. As a result, feelings are produced, depending on what went into the test tube. As we have addressed previously, your thoughts, experiences, expectations, and nearly everything else influence your feelings. There are numerous other 'ingredients' that sometimes go unnoticed, but that have a strong impact on your state of mind. Here are just a few of them.

SLEEP   FOOD   COMMUNICATION

| + | + | = JOY

| + | + | = ANGER

| + | + | = SADNESS

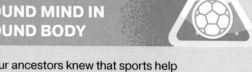

A SOUND MIND IN A SOUND BODY

Even our ancestors knew that sports help cheer people up and reduce their stress levels. However, only recently were scientists able to explain why. When you participate in sports, your blood circulation improves, and substances that have a positive effect on brain performance get produced. The more actively and regularly you participate in sports, the more visible the effect is. Right after physical activity your head will become clearer, and your spirits higher. What's more, being physically active helps you process information and cope with stress.

SLEEPING THE RIGHT WAY

If you haven't had enough sleep, you're sure to feel anxiety and irritation. If you've had too much sleep, you're sure to develop indifference and positive emotions will be dimmed. What can you do about this? Get the right amount of sleep. Aim to get no less than 8, but no more than 10 hours of sleep a day. Your lights-out and wake-up times are also important. Staying active late at night and sleeping until lunchtime is a bad idea. There is an invisible clock in your body that needs to correspond to the alternation of day and night, or your moods will bounce from high to low.

BURNING THE MIDNIGHT OIL

If your daily regimen goes off track, hormone production gets disturbed, too. That is why positive experiences are felt less intensely. And the less joy you feel during the day, the more you want to extend pleasure late at night when you are free of your obligations. Endless browsing through the internet or watching an entire season of a TV series in one go is bad for your health as well as for your mood. You will feel battered the next morning, while your day and evening will follow the same path, and you will end up in a vicious cycle.

YOU ARE WHAT YOU EAT

Yes, indeed. Your body needs energy not only for growing, moving, and learning, but also for coping with any stress. Hunger intensifies nervousness. At the same time, if you eat too much, you become sleepy and lethargic. It's important to maintain a balance and eat exactly what is needed to maintain your level of activity (including mental activity).

Hunger may intensify when you're going through unpleasant experiences or agitation. Many people try to offset that with sweets or fast food.
The brain makes the switch to pleasure mode when we eat. But this pleasure passes quickly, and the negative consequences remain. Before filling up your stomach with unhealthy food, contemplate why you want to eat this junk. Is it worth it?

DAILY REGIMEN ADULTS TALK SO MUCH ABOUT

It's really important. When you have little sleep, little food, and not enough physical activity, and you stay up late with a smartphone in your hand, your body physically has no resources to feel good. And when you're physically under par, your mood will adjust correspondingly.

DOES IT MATTER WITH WHOM YOU TALK?

You are the mathematical mean of the five people you spend time with regularly. When in the company of active people, you become active and energetic. On the contrary, when those with zero desire for anything surround you, you lose interest in life quickly. Be careful with your choice of friends. Ask yourself, "Do I want to be like them?" Read about mirror neurons on page 98!

That is why it's recommended that you fill your mornings and afternoons with physical activity, so that you will feel pleasantly tired by the evening.

IS IT POSSIBLE TO MIX DIFFERENT INGREDIENTS ON PURPOSE TO INFLUENCE YOUR MOOD?

For sure! Experiment if you already know what influences your mood and what effect it produces! This way you will develop your own formula for happiness, vigor, and tranquility.

TIPS TO FIGURE OUT WHAT GOT MIXED IN YOUR TEST TUBE TODAY

Turn on your observer mode more often and ask yourself:

? What exactly am I feeling? In which part of my body does this emotion live?

? How late was I up last night?

? Am I hungry? Or just the opposite?

? When exactly did I feel like eating something? Does it have anything to do with my agitation or some unpleasant experiences?

? Can my location influence my mood?

YOUR FORMULA FOR JOY

What Emotions Does My Body Trigger?

Do you look in the mirror and realize you don't recognize yourself? Just a while ago you didn't care about your appearance. Why is it all different now? And how is it connected to your emotions?

Most likely you're at the age that people call puberty, or sexual maturation. You no longer have a child's body — you're turning into an adult, even though you may not see physical signs yet. Here are just a few changes that your body is working on. Your nose and ears are becoming larger. You're getting acne and your hair becomes oily and dirty more quickly. Course hairs begin appearing up and down your body. Your hands and feet are growing more quickly than your trunk.

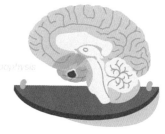

hypophysis

All of these (and many other) changes occur due to the activation of once-dormant **sex hormones**. They were triggered by the hypophysis, the central organ of your endocrine system and the 'head honcho' of all hormones. Its main function is to initiate the rebuilding of your body in time to prepare you for adult life.

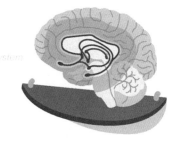

limbic system

Your brain is under the influence of sex hormones too: the limbic system, which is responsible for emotions, is working at full capacity. Meanwhile, the frontal lobe, which is responsible for planning and control, is still under development. That is why your moods may swing from euphoria to apathy in split seconds.

WHAT IS HAPPENING TO MY EMOTIONS?

Have you become touchy and easily upset? Is everything driving you mad? You can thank puberty for this, too. Your body is now spending a lot of energy on growth and transformation. An awful lot of energy! That is why it sometimes lacks the capacity to cope with an inflow of feelings. When you are physically tired, and your energy is at zero, it's especially difficult to control your behavior.

WHY AM I NOT INTERESTED IN ANYTHING AND GET BORED SO QUICKLY?

Starting from infancy, your brain has been constantly building millions of neural connections. Now some of them are disconnecting (that's because you don't use all of them), while new ones take longer to be established. That is why you may grow cold to your former hobbies, even if you've had them for years and been good at them. The same may be said about your studies.

I hate my body

Nearly every teenager is uncomfortable with his or her body, even people you consider to be very beautiful. That's a fact! It's important to remember the following:

That beauty is in the eye of the beholder. Ask 100 people, and everyone will have a unique opinion on what beauty is. That's why there's no point in trying to adapt yourself to some standard that doesn't even exist.

Your current body is not its final version. Don't hurry to dismiss yourself as too thin/thick, or too short/tall. A lot of what you consider a problem will go away on its own.

Tips to accepting your body and your beauty

Pay attention to other people's beauty. Note that what you like in people is always something special or unique. The most attractive people don't always look like cover models, but rather have some sort of charisma.

Focus on opportunities your body offers. Sense what happens in your body when you're singing, drawing, or running. Does your body feel good? Do you feel positive energy? Yes, your body can feel fine regardless of what you think about it!

Find your own special flavor and something you like about yourself. Pay more attention to this feature, accentuate it by dressing in a certain way. Being unique is more important than fitting a mold.

Stop comparing yourself to others, especially to 'beauty icons' from social networks and TV ads. Another person's beauty should never stand in the way of you manifesting your own charm. You don't have to compete, and there's no prize to be won.

Remind yourself time and again that **you are more than just a body.** Your beliefs, aspirations, and actions are what really matter.

Is it going to last?

Don't worry, your raging hormones will gradually level out, your body realignment will be completed, and your brain will find a balance. **Show some patience, wisdom, and compassion to yourself** and your dramatic changes.

What's Next?

Things to keep in mind

- What emotions are your most frequent hide-and-seek partners?
- How do you usually react when you are overwhelmed by an intense feeling?
- Whom do you most frequently hear in your mind: a detractor or a supporter?
- Follow your emotional state throughout the day: what has had an influence on you?
- What are your inner sources of joy and happiness?

Your tools

- Gratitude exercises
- A daily regimen that suits you
- Meditation

Worth reading

- Tina Rae. **It's OK Not to Be OK: A Guide to Wellbeing**
- Tanya Richardson. **Zen Teen: 40 Ways to Stay Calm When Life Gets Stressful**

Worth watching

Tim Urban.
Inside the mind of a master procrastinator

David Staindl-Rast.
Want to be happy? Be grateful

CHAPTER 5

What Do Others Feel?

Does understanding yourself mean understanding others?

We learn to understand our feelings not just because we want to be at peace with ourselves. We are surrounded by people just like us. Understanding their emotions is key to communication, friendship, and love.

How do we understand others?

When your friend has a problem, you feel sad too. When your mom really likes the present you gave her, you share her joy.

In all these situations, you use a special gift called **empathy**, which allows you to understand **what exactly another person feels and experiences**. Empathy has been developing in mankind for ages, which has helped us to survive collectively. It is considered a key quality of future generations.

Different levels of empathy

Everyone has a different empathy level, from low (you can barely figure out what another person is feeling) to high (you experience another person's feelings just like your own). What empathy level do you think you have? You can use the questions below to find it out:

 Do you always scan another person's emotion?

 How much are you influenced by another person's feeling?

 Are you able to share somebody's joy or sadness?

Is empathy enough?

Empathy helps you understand what others feel. This is the first step to meeting another person halfway. However, **empathy alone is not enough** to resolve problems together or help each other. You need one more attribute capable of turning you from a spectator of the movie called life into one of its protagonists. **What we're talking about is kindness.** When you understood another person's feelings and are able to show kindness, you are feeling compassion.

Why should I care about others?

The world is a mirror. It gives back what you offer it. If you want to live in peace and enjoy other people's support, you should be compassionate with them and help them.

TIPS TO MASTERING COMPASSION

GET OUT OF YOUR COMFORT ZONE

Our ability to understand people who are different is limited by our own experience. If we are unfamiliar with a situation, then our heart remains locked.

Maybe a friend has broken his arm and you don't know how it feels? Ask him or her and try to experience his or her pain together.

LOOK FOR THE REASON

If you're mad at something somebody has done, or if you don't understand that person at all, ask yourself, "Why has he or she acted this way? What drove him or her to do this?" There is a reason behind everything.

FEELINGS BRING US TOGETHER

No matter how different our experience and situations may be, we are all united by feelings. We are all experience fear, pain, joy, and curiosity from time to time. Focus on the feelings of the person who is in need of compassion.
Ask yourself, "How would I feel if I were in his or her shoes?"

TURN OFF THE CRITIC

Listen and observe keenly but reserve your judgment. Judging and blaming put you back in your safe spot and make you blind to other people's experiences.
When we judge and blame others, it's just like we are denying them the right to their feelings. Imagine others treating your feelings as nonsense. What would you think about that?

ACCEPT ANOTHER PERSON'S RIGHT TO BE

Compassion means acknowledging everyone's right to be who he or she wants to be. Everyone is unique, just like you are. Everybody has the right to be respected, just like you do.

BE PROACTIVE

If you want to support somebody, make sure you ask him, "How can I help?" and listen to what he has to say. Very often people need support and someone who will just listen, which can make a big difference.

EMPATHY + KINDNESS = COMPASSION

Compassion literally means being able to share somebody's passion, which means treating your troubles and other peoples' troubles the same — and truly being ready to help.

Compassion lies at the core of human morals and should be the basis of any human relations. Currently, the world is learning to be compassionate in hopes of avoiding future destructive wars and conflicts.

How to Speak About Your Feelings

Figuring out your feelings is not an easy task. But it is even more difficult for others to understand what you are feeling. Is there a way to talk about your emotions so that you enhance, rather than ruin your relations with someone?

Use this special formula:
'I-message'

WHY IS IT SO DIFFICULT TO TALK ABOUT YOUR FEELINGS?

False convictions and negative experiences stand in the way.

- You have talked candidly about your emotions but failed to reach a mutual understanding.
- You are afraid that your loved ones will be hurt or upset if you tell them about your honest feelings.
- In your family it just isn't customary to talk about feelings.

When you talk about your emotions, you're not being weak or egotistic. What you want is to improve relations with a person and not hurt anyone. That's why there's no reason to be embarrassed. Quite the opposite, there's a reason to be proud: **it takes courage to open up to people**.

I AM/FEEL

When you say 'I', you assume responsibility for your experience. This is a brave thing to do and deserves respect.

EMOTION

Describe your emotion, as people around you may have no idea what you're feeling.

WHEN

Provide a clear description of the situation in which you started feeling this way.

BECAUSE

Explain why you think this is so important and how an act or statement by another person is connected to what you feel.

We often speak as if somebody is in control of our emotions, and we rush to blame others for what we are feeling.
"You've offended me," "It's all because of you," "Your tone ticks me off!" Saying such things is a sure way to lose mutual understanding.

It hurt me when you decided to go out with that other group, **even though** you and I had already agreed to go out together.

I waited for you when I could have gone out with my other friends.

I got angry when you interrupted me. I felt it was important to tell you this story.

Please try not to interrupt me again.

I got upset when you told everyone that I failed my entrance exam to music school.

I asked you not to share this with anyone. You promised you wouldn't. I trusted you.

Never let it happen again

> Please just give me a hug. It's really important to me.

It's very easy: **just tell the person who upset you that there is a better way to treat you**. Or explain how he or she can support you. Do you want that person to apologize? Or do you just want a hug from him or her? Do you want to be left alone? Do you want the person to let you know in advance if plans have changed? Just tell him or her straight up!

It's where and how you say it

If you fly off the handle, hardly anyone would want to listen to what you have to say. Speak quietly and take your time. Think about whether you want to discuss the issue here and now. Is there a place where you would be more comfortable? Would it be better to wait until your emotions subside? **Your goal is not to argue, but to set the record straight and express what you are feeling**.

Other ways to show your discontent

Use secret codes
They will show your friends and family that you're out of your element. Just agree with them beforehand what word or action to use as a code.

> Do the dishes!

> **Sir, yes sir!**

> I'm angry as hell.

> I am not happy with this at all.

> I am really ticked off.

> Sorry, I didn't mean to sound bossy. Could you please do the dishes when you have some free time?

> But I don't want to talk right now. Let's do it later. When would it work for you?

This is your secret code. It shows that you don't like getting orders instead of being asked.

Take a time out
When you're too tired to talk, when you're afraid of saying too much, or when you see that the other party is nervous and may have a meltdown, offer the person a chance to **take a break**.

It's not working anyway

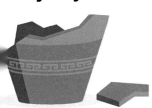

Is your friend unwilling to listen when you speak about your feelings? Unfortunately, not everyone is ready to build honest balanced relations. Always bear in mind that **you're only responsible for your own actions, your own feelings, and the methods you use to express them**. How others react is their responsibility, not yours. If you find that others are unable to grasp why you are unhappy, try not to get upset. You have every right to speak about the things that you like or dislike!

Giving and Getting Feedback

At times it can be quite difficult to understand one another! One careless word may be enough to unleash a storm of emotions. How can you speak and hear the other person's words, while remaining an observer?

Why do we get offended?

When our deepest and most basic wishes — also known as our needs — do not align with another person's needs, or he/she is left unsatisfied, conflicts and arguments arise.

Rule of thumb for any conversation:

Our posture and body language, and our choice of words (HOW we say things) are no less important than the actual message (WHAT we say). Sometimes these differences may define how the other person will respond.

For example, you're tearing your hair out because your friend is late. Your need for respect is being ignored. But are you absolutely sure that your friend lost respect for you? Or maybe he or she was a bit busy?

Think about your own needs and the other person's needs when you are in a troubling situation. It's much more interesting than simply getting offended and angry about what's on the surface.

FEEDBACK FORMULA

You listen but don't always hear what the other person says and means. And vice versa.

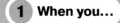

1 **When you…** (the other person's action)

2 **I feel…** (your emotion)

3 **Because…** (your need)

4 **Now you understand why…** (your emotion)

Examples

When you were late (**1**), I got very angry (**2**). It seemed to me you don't give a damn about me (**3**). Do you see now why I get mad when people are late (**4**)?

When you tell me to clean my room (**1**), I get irritated (**2**). I start feeling like a little boy who is not allowed to make any decisions (**3**). Do you see now why I am responding in such a rude manner (**4**)? By the way, why do you care whether my room is clean or not?

Three of our most common perception mistakes

1

THAT'S NOT TRUE!

A person's words seem terribly unfair. For example, Dad says, "You never have time for us!" Even though you went to a football game with him just last weekend.

WHAT'S THE PROBLEM?

Such feedback is too generic. Words like "never," "always," or "all you do is..." are not specific. At the same time, they give the impression that the other person does not differentiate between behavior and personality, as if behavior is personality. This is always hurtful!

SOLUTION:

- Ask what the other person means.
- Don't use generic words when you speak about the other person's behavior.
- Remember, it's on you if you get offended about things that other people say.

2

IT'S ALL YOUR FAULT!

You are looking for someone to blame. For instance, you tell your friend, "We're late for school because of you."

WHAT'S THE PROBLEM?

- You shift responsibility for your actions onto some other person.
- You believe that the truth is always on your side.

SOLUTION:

- Don't blame others for your own mistakes.
- Look at the other person's actions through his or her eyes.
- Discuss everyone's areas of responsibility in every situation and come up with an action plan for the future.

3

IS THERE SOMETHIGN WRONG WITH ME?

It may seem that words can jeopardize our own views of ourselves. Most often this is how we react to criticism, no matter how mild it is. For example, Mom says, "You're looking scraggly again! Why is it so difficult for you to brush your hair?"

WHAT'S THE PROBLEM?

- You feel like you're being attacked personally, and not the issue involving you.
- It looks like a person close to you doesn't love you and is treating you terribly.

SOLUTION:

- Separate your words from your feelings about a person. Do you really think your Mom doesn't love you? Or is she just trying to help by showing you that she cares?
- Find the courage to laugh at yourself and admit that you're not always perfect at everything you do.
- Derive some benefit from criticism: look at the situation through the other person's eyes (turn on your observer mode) and look for some meaning in the advice you've been given.
  - Think about the reasons why that person is giving you this advice. Are his or her intentions good or ill-willed?

Be careful when you choose the time and place for feedback — make sure the other person is ready to listen and hear what you have to say. If you use the feedback properly, there will never be unresolvable conflicts in your life.

Figuring Out a Friend's Feelings

"What, is he angry with me?" "She is avoiding me." "Why don't we hang out anymore?" It would be great to have a dedicated translation machine to interpret other people's feelings, wouldn't it? Such a machine actually exists inside you. But you must pass a few levels to activate it, just like in a computer game.

FAMILY COMMUNICATION

EXPERIENCE

PHYSICAL CONDITION

GENETICS

RULES OF SOCIETY

A friend's feelings might be different from yours

Over a lifetime you go through a lot of experiences and learn to react to each of them in a unique way. This happens to everybody. **But experience is only one of numerous factors that influence how we feel.**

It's no wonder that we all feel and express emotions in our own way! If you come across a bewildering emotion or its manifestation, don't get irritated or blame anyone for feeling it. It makes more sense to try come to terms with it!

LEVEL 1
Body language

Gestures, posture, facial expressions — everything that is called **body language** — will help you decode what your friend is feeling.

YOUR FRIEND IS CALM, SHE FEELS HAPPY AND SAFE:
Open posture, gesturing hands, a smile on her face, slow movements, she is looking you in the eye, her voice is ringing, and her body is relaxed.

YOUR FRIEND IS CONCERNED AND INSECURE:
Her arms are folded, she is looking away, her movements are agitated, she is frequently nodding or blinking, her body is turned to one side, her voice is muffled, even if she is smiling, she is touching her face or squeezing her own hands.

LEVEL 2
Word

Whoa!

What's up

Doh!

Friends may say hurtful things, yell, ignore, or avoid us — **behind all of this is emotional pain**.

When a person is only just learning how to express what he or she is experiencing, communication turns into a maze of hints and guesses.

All of us, even adults, are still wandering through this labyrinth. How can you navigate it?

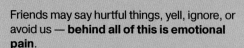

LOOK FOR THE ROOT CAUSE

Feelings do not emerge from out of nowhere, **they always have a root cause**. We often fail to say (and sometimes even fail to understand) what specifically gave birth to a particular emotion, we just let it burst out.
For example, when your friend says, "I am sick and tired of everything," there must be some unpleasant situation that pushed her to this point. Ask her what happened.

Sometimes signals from a friend are so subtle that it seems impossible to understand what they could mean.
In this case, use a simple and effective tool — **direct questions!**
Don't hesitate to ask openly and kindly what's going on:

BONUS LEVEL

"Are you upset about something?"
"I see that something's wrong. What is it?"
"Are you sure you like doing this?"
Demonstrate your sincere interest and a desire to get to the bottom of the issue — this is THE KEY to reaching an understanding!

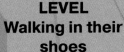

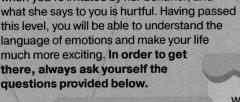

The most complicated level is **learning to put yourself in your friend's shoes**. Especially when you're irritated by her behavior, and what she says to you is hurtful. Having passed this level, you will be able to understand the language of emotions and make your life much more exciting. **In order to get there, always ask yourself the questions provided below.**

What drives your friend? What does she want/not want?

3 LEVEL
Walking in their shoes

How would you react in this situation? Why would you react this way?

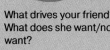

Is there at least one reason why your friend is behaving this way? Maybe it's beyond your communication (something has happened in her family or at school).

Ouch!

PLAYING THE OBSERVER
To have a better understanding of other people's feelings

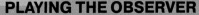

SURE WAY TO FAILURE:
Snowballing the misunderstanding, grievance, anger, and stewing over the problem will only create and widen the gap between you.

CHALLENGE 1:
Take note of your posture (both yours and hers), follow the body language of the person you are talking to and try to guess what she is feeling.

CHALLENGE 2:
If you have spotted an interesting person in some situation, try to feel what she might be feeling at that moment.

Sometimes this gap can grow very quickly, even if there is no real reason for it existing in the first place.
Don't do the thinking for the other person, but rather speak about your own feelings and ask your friend about hers.

LOOK FOR A NEED

Everybody wants something: to be liked, avoid loneliness, or have friends. Look for the need hidden in your friend's words. For example, she got offended and was unwilling to talk to you because you didn't invite her to have lunch. The desire to be needed is what is hiding behind her grievance. Tell her that you value her and explain the reason for your choice.

What Do Your Parents Feel?

Yes, indeed, they have feelings, too. Any parent is a regular human being, not a superman or a monster. What your parents do and what they demand of you often seems absurd to you, but it may be driven by their feelings and emotions. What if we get to the bottom of what drives them?

Parents are human too!

Wouldn't it be perfect to have a robot as a parent, always accepting of everything and relaxed... Or maybe not? If this were the case, we would not receive much love from them! **Your parents, just like you, experience all kinds of feelings, both pleasant and unpleasant.** Anger, bitterness, fear — all emotions are familiar to them and influence their mood and behavior.

Back in the day, it was a common belief that emotions were a manifestation of weakness and that it was improper to show them. Most present-day parents grew up with that paradigm. That is why your dad may believe that men don't cry, and mom may be sure that girls must learn to grin and bear it.

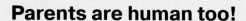

What drives your parents' emotions?

Things that they need to get done that either turn out fine or quite the opposite — their work, friends, household chores... all of which may have nothing to do with you. But sometimes the emotions they express as adults about these things may affect you as well. Imagine that an intense emotion such as anger is a bucket full of water that an adult is forced to carry around the house. It is only a matter of time before some of the anger will spill out.

Parental duties that they carry out on a daily basis. When these duties are a pleasure, parents definitely enjoy themselves. But when they turn into a burden, parents may grow upset or get annoyed, start to blame themselves or get downright angry.

We sometimes attribute some feelings (or the absence thereof) to our parents, but **the cause may be somewhere else**. You may think your mum doesn't love you. But she is just tired after a long day at work.

Your achievements or failures concern your parents too. They are proud of your progress and upset when you step out of line.

How do adults commonly deal with their feelings and emotions? They…

Suppress them and keep them inside — that is the most common method for dealing with unpleasant emotions. After these feelings have reached critical mass, they will sooner or later burst out. This is called an emotional breakdown.

Manifest them in words and actions. But adults don't always do this constructively. When an adult says, "Put on your winter hat," in a strict voice, it may seem that they're expressing anger, when in fact it's just their way of showing concern.

Sometimes adults are controversial in their actions — they may praise you and take you apart at the same time, they may be quiet and fly off the handle in a matter of minutes.
This is all because parents, too, are not always aware of their feelings. Most likely they've never been told what to do about their feelings.

Tips to understanding parents

Parents' demands may seem illogical and groundless at times. But each one has a valid reason. What's the key to understanding your parents?

Trust, transparency, and communication will help:

Ask your parents about the reasons why they want things done a certain way, making sure your question is in the proper form.

Share your feelings with your parents, rather than hide or suppress them. Team up with them to find ways of expressing emotions that would be acceptable to everyone in your family.

You all need to communicate in order to understand each other. Don't close the door on spending time together, taking shared trips, or doing activities. They will help you avoid months of tense standoffs.

Be honest about what is at the core of your emotions, and about what you think the causes of their emotions are. Speak clearly and avoid insults.

Not recommended:

"You don't care about me, and you don't take my interests seriously!" (Exits, slams the door.)

Recommended:

"I am upset because you don't allow me to visit my friends in the evening. I'd like to know your reasons. Is there a way I can gain your trust and get your permission?"

4 ESSENTIAL DON'Ts

1
DON'T put your parents on a pedestal and expect them to be correct in all situations.

2
DON'T judge your parents for their way of handling emotions, rather help them by asking questions and setting an example.

3
DON'T take to heart every emotion, feeling, or sentiment that your parents may have.

4
DON'T be afraid to be yourself and show your emotions.

Keep in mind that no matter what your parents may be feeling at a particular moment, and no matter how weird their demands may seem to you, love for you is at the core of their actions.

Expressing Love and Care — Learn the Language

Chances are that you've studied a foreign language at one time or another. It's a very common thing to do if you want to understand people from other countries. It turns out that your friends and family may be a bit foreign to you as well, and understanding them requires that you speak their language, the language of love!

What kind of special language is that?

Author and philosopher Gary Chapman defined five different ways of expressing love and care, which he called five love languages. A person usually "speaks" one of them, perhaps two. A relationship is solid if the people involved understand both their language and the language of a partner, friend, or relative.

Language 1. Words of affirmation

You use words to communicate your love, to show the other person that he's valid and important.

How can you communicate this?
Just speak! Encourage and affirm the other person's actions or thoughts, appreciate them, and express your requests in a gentle manner.

For example:
"That story you told was great."

I want to tell you a story...

Language 2. Physical touch

A native speaker of this language needs physical contact to feel support and love. This is a popular language, as it's the primary language of most children who are under the age of five. But it's not limited to that age group. Many adults speak this language, too.

How can you communicate this?
Hug, touch, hold hands, stay close to each other.

For example:
Hug your mom or dad before going to school every morning.

Language 3. Acts of service

You must have heard the saying "Actions speak louder than words." It was definitely coined by a person who regards acts of service as his or her main love language. Those who speak through acts of service expect you to express your love by doing something for someone.

How can you communicate this?
Manifest your care and affection in actions that will be valued by a specific person, that he or she would love to do together with someone, or receive as a service.

For example:
Has your dad just returned from shopping? Help him sort out the shopping bags.

What's your language?

There are several ways to discover which language is easiest for you to understand.

- Ask yourself the following questions: How is it that you know your parents truly love you? What in your communications with friends or family members can hurt you? Is it something that they do or don't do? Or something they say or don't say? What is it you need to receive from your parents or friends most often?
- Think about how you express your love and affection: is it through words, actions, gifts, touching, or time spent with them? The answer will most likely be your primary love language.

Tips to figuring out another person's language

The simplest way is to ask! Tell your friends about this concept and ask them to decide which language is theirs. A more difficult way is to monitor your friends and family closely. What makes them happy, and what makes them sad? How do they express their love? This way you can quickly figure out which language is best for communicating with them.

Language 4. Gift giving

This language is the easiest to learn! There's no difficult dialect here, just give your friends or family something they would enjoy receiving.

How can you communicate this?
Give gifts. You don't always have to buy them. You can make, draw, or cook them on your own. Any gift will do, even a small one. The most important thing is giving it without expecting anything in return, but with a solid understanding of the other person's needs.

For example:
Leave a note for your parents with some words of love or a drawing.

Language 5. Quality time

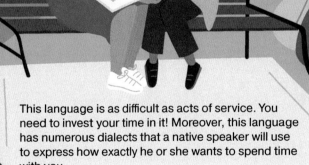

This language is as difficult as acts of service. You need to invest your time in it! Moreover, this language has numerous dialects that a native speaker will use to express how exactly he or she wants to spend time with you.

How can you communicate this?
The most important thing is to dedicate some time to your loved one unconditionally and completely. From there, everything depends on the dialect he or she speaks: some value lengthy in-depth conversations when you don't get distracted by gadgets, while others are interested in activities that you can do together. There are also some who will be happy just to sit with you in complete silence.

For example:
Visit your grandma, look through old photo albums with her, and listen to her stories.

Mending a Friendship When You're Both Hurt

Being friends is not always easy. We get offended, we find fault in a friend, we experience a sudden cooling of relations — and often for no reason, or so it seems. Well, that's not quite the case. It's just that we don't always succeed in sharing our feelings. Is there anything you can do?

Start with yourself

Psychologist Eric Berne gave the world a very useful model that ties interpersonal relationships to one of three ego-states of the individuals involved: the **Child ego**, **Parent ego** or the **Adult ego** states. They change from one situation to the next, regardless of the individual's actual age. Your parents, teachers, friends, as well as you, are always alternating between these three states!

Parent ego state

This state is triggered when it is necessary to manage someone, or when we believe that others can't do something without us. It's often the state in which we give unsolicited advice, try too hard to be clever, or become both poor listeners and deaf to criticism.

How do your parents behave in various situations? In which instances do you start behaving just like them?

Child ego state

This is a dual state. It comes in handy when you are surprised and excited, or when you want to try new things and just enjoy yourself. It also stands in your way when you start acting up, when you don't want to listen to anybody and only think about yourself, or when you become touchy and let your emotions take over.

Think about the times when you indeed turn into a child. For example, does this happen to you when parents expect you to assist them with household chores? Do your friends or even your teachers revert to this state as well from time to time?

Ask your friends to elaborate on what exactly upsets and hurts them about your behavior. Remember their words and try to change something in your behavior before you demand that others change their ways.

Even if your friends' responses cause you pain, remember about the Adult inside and make sure you don't revert to the Child state. Speak honestly about the way you feel, using the 'I-message' formula (see page 84).

Align with your friends so that you all have a common view of the situation.

Ask clarifying questions: are you sure you understand correctly what the other person meant?

Ask your friends to explain what has happened. This will immediately put them in Adult state thinking.

Learn to identify the state in which your friends are at the moment. For instance, are they yelling in an attempt to make their case? This is the bossy Parent state. How would you react? You will surely be tempted to act like the Child and become defensive. But will this help bring back mutual understanding?

Tips to helping a friend become an Adult

Listen to your friend earnestly and attentively. Don't get distracted by your phone, don't interrupt, and don't offer unsolicited advice.

Adult ego state

This is the wisest and most balanced state. An Adult respects another person's feelings and is ready to ask questions and listen. And Adult ego would not go to extremes and will be willing to find a mutually beneficial solution for both parties. A person in this state is an observer, one who understands his or her feelings, as well as other people's feelings.

When are you in the Adult ego state?

Don't make excuses, don't become defensive, and don't make your case too aggressively. First of all, try to get to the bottom of the situation, like a calm and collected observer would do.

If the Child just won't go away, shift your focus. For example, ask yourself, "What feeling is currently overwhelming me?" Sense the floor under your feet, pay attention to your physical sensations.

Stop and take a break. Figure out which of the three states you are in at the moment. This very realization will put you in the Adult state.

Tips to being the Adult in your conversations

Does 'Different' Mean 'Dangerous'?

Look around, there are so many different people! Some of them are like you, while others are not. There are those who feel the same as you do, and those who see the world in a different light. There are those who have a different skin color. Or those who speak a language you don't understand. There are those who are confined to a wheelchair or those who can't speak or hear at all. What is the proper way to treat 'different' people? Should they receive special treatment?

Do I feel the same as you?

All of us have the same feelings. But we may express them differently. The less a person is similar to you, the bigger the difference is. Is he or she from a different country, part of a different religion, or subject to different societal and/or family rules? Does he or she belong to a different race, speak a different language, or have body features different than yours? Answering yes to just one of the above questions is sufficient for a person to express his or her emotions and act differently.

Then and now

In ancient times, when people waged war for survival, it was common to be hostile toward outsiders. People would differentiate between 'us' and 'them' based on appearances. Our brains would follow a simple pattern: if they look like us, they are friends, and if they look different, they are foes. Being lefthanded was enough for a person to be considered an 'outsider'! This ingrained pattern was justified back then. Such thinking now stands in the way of cooperation and human development, both of which benefit from the melding of many different cultural views and approaches. Furthermore, such a mindset does not allow you to see the person behind the differences.

⚡ What is xenophobia?

Fear or hatred of 'outsiders' is called xenophobia. Anybody who is significantly different is perceived as an enemy. This worldview is a collection of all the most negative feelings:

- ⚡ **mistrust** in outsiders
- ☁ **anxiety and fear** of their doing harm
- 💧 **contempt and disgust** for being different
- ⚡ **sense of superiority**
- ☁ **hostility and hatred**

Different but equal

You can have another worldview altogether, one that is colorful and full of admiration of the variety and uniqueness of humanity. What about dogs? A Great Dane would never consider staying clear of some odd-looking bulldog, and the same would be true for a dachshund and a St. Bernard, no matter how strikingly different they are in size, color, or breed. This view is called **inclusivity**, meaning that you understand that the world has a place for everyone, no matter how 'different' he or she may be.

Respect and empathy for people, regardless of their skin color, appearance, health status, abilities, or religion is the basic premise of tolerance and one of the main values of today's world.

Tolerance is not a fashion or a matter of taste. It is an important condition for the development of society and for bringing people together. It is a path towards harmony and happiness, serving as an antidote to xenophobia and racism.

Stereotypes are evolutionary relics trapped in peoples' thought patterns. They are like garden weeds that have deep roots but are detrimental to the garden itself.

Stereotypes and feelings

Some may believe that all people with autism or Down syndrome are odd. Or that all people of a specific nationality are evil or primitive. Ideas like these are called **negative stereotypes**, which breed xenophobia.

WHAT CONSTITUTES A STEREOTYPE:

human category name:
deaf people... Asians... etc.

+

traits attributed to them: unwelcome, sneaky, aggressive, etc.

=

negative emotions and feelings

Meeting an 'outsider'

Remember: a human life has unconditional value. This value is the same for any life; there is nobody who is more valuable than another person, for whatever reason. Therefore, everyone in the world has the right to be who he or she wants to be.

Fear, anxiety and aggression against 'outsiders' are caused by ignorance. Try to establish contact with an 'outsider'. You can do this by going to see a play starring physically challenged people or by starting a nice conversation with one of your peers of a different nationality whom you previously ignored. You will see that most of your apprehensions and preconceptions about the person will turn out to be unwarranted and unnecessary.

★ **See a person primarily for the person he or she is, not as an 'outsider'.** Focus on the things you have in common, not on those areas where you differ.

★ **Offer your help if it is needed, but don't show pity or condescension.** Helping people with motor, sight, hearing, or other impairments is as natural as helping an elderly lady to cross the street.

★ **Practice looking at the world through other people's eyes more often** — especially when it comes to those who are different. When you put yourself in other people's shoes, get a feel for their joys and tribulations, as well as their opportunities and limitations. Sense your inner connection with people, as you and all other people are part of the same social organism. Can you imagine that a part of an organism would hate and resent another part?

Sharing Feelings

Did you know that not all of your feelings are entirely yours? Some feelings are like air that is being breathed simultaneously by several people, a team, a city, or even an entire country. Sometimes 'inhaling' shared emotions and feelings does you good. Other times you are better off avoiding them.

A recent discovery has shed light on how **mirror neurons** enable us not only to understand, but also experience the emotions of a person in close proximity to us or even repeat his or her actions. Sometimes we act like a receiver and capture those feelings that are hanging in the air.

Recall your own experience with shared feelings in your family, a group of friends, with classmates, or on a sports team.

STRONGER TOGETHER

Nature endowed us with shared feelings to stand up against imminent danger, so that we can survive an earthquake or team up to deal with a natural disaster. We are stronger together, and not only physically. Cooperation is an efficient mechanism that is vital for peaceful purposes in times of peace.

WHAT FEELINGS ARE SHARED MOST OFTEN?

SHARED ANGER

Several people are angry at somebody or something. Students are angry at a teacher who has given them a surprise test. One sports team is angry at another to whom they have recently lost a game.

SHAREED HATRED

Several people denounce and reject a person. A teenage gang decides to torture a homeless cat. Fans of a sports team choose to hate the fans of another sports team.

Shared anger and hatred are very dangerous emotions. When they are reproduced, they feed off the energy of every person in the group. With the support of a mob, all members believe that their emotion is justified and reasonable.

However, it is a fact that at a certain point mobs stop seeing reality. When people speak about mobs being under the influence of such emotions, they often refer to participants as being 'blinded by rage'. Aggression can reach the level when a mob might start doing harm to others.

Examples: an entire class chooses to bully one of their classmates. Or when fans of different sports clubs have fist fights with each other.

SHARED FEAR

Several people feel threatened and in danger simultaneously. They may be tourists in nature suddenly stricken by a natural disaster, or an entire class right before they are about to take a tough exam. If shared, very intense fear may result in panic.

SHARED JOY

People are having fun and enjoying themselves together at a family celebration or during a game. Such joy can be shared by a much greater number of people, like several thousand spectators at a concert or a sporting event.

THE LORD OF COLLECTIVE EMOTIONS

Who can control the emotions of a team? It's the team's leader. He or she is the one who can influence others, and to whom team members will listen, agree with, and will respect as a role model. This person may amplify some shared emotions and weaken others. What if you are the leader? Keep an eye on how the leader influences the overall mood of the class.

Tips to differentiating emotions

It's not always clear which emotions are your own, and which come from the group. If you distance yourself too much from your team, you may miss out on shared joy or success.

At the same time, if you always give in to the collective vibe, you might get infected with unpleasant emotions such as anger, hate, or fear. What should you do?

Be an observer. Pay attention to what others feel. Try to figure out where these emotions come from, and how they influence people's actions and their overall mood.

Ask yourself, "Do I want to experience these feelings collectively with everybody?" If the answer is yes, join in and enjoy yourself. Emotions are most intense when we can share them with others.

If the answer is no, try not to follow the crowd. Keep an eye on your body's sensations. They will let you know whether you have come under the influence of collective emotions.

Compare people's actions to your own values. No matter what kind of fun a group or team promises, step aside if you consider it wrong or inappropriate.

If anger or hate is directed at you, tell yourself, "It's just their emotions, it has nothing to do with me." Remember that a shared feeling does not necessarily reflect reality.

Imagine that these people are infected with a dangerous emotional ailment from which they will surely recover.

If you must face shared aggression, make sure you seek help from those individuals who can put a stop to it, meaning your parents, teachers, or brothers and sisters. If you're protecting yourself, there's nothing to be ashamed of!

What's Next?

Things to keep in mind

- Whom do you empathize with most often? Why?

- Think of some lesser-known person who is different from you. Try to look at the world through this person's eyes, imagine what his or her life is like.

- Were you successful in understanding him or her better?

- Were you able to feel real empathy and compassion?

- What's your main love language?

- What experience do you have with shared feelings in class, your family, and among friends? What shared feelings do you prefer to stay away from?

Worth reading

- Gary Chapman. **The Five Love Languages**
- Eric Berne. **Games People Play**

Brene Brown.
The power of vulnerability

Worth watching

Simon Sinek.
How great leaders inspire action

Robert Waldinger.
What makes a good life

References

Chapter 1. What Exactly Are Feelings?

1. Lisa Feldman Barrett. **How Emotions Are Made. The Secret Life of the Brain.** — London: Pan Books, 2018.

2. Travis Bradberry. **Emotional Intelligence 2.0.** — San Diego: TalentSmart, 2009.

3. Daniel Goleman. **Emotional Intelligence: Why It Can Matter More Than IQ.** — NYC: Bantam Books, 1995.

4. Ilse Sand. **The Emotional Compass.** — London: Jessica Kingsley Pub., 2016.

5. Kerrie Fleming. **The Leader's Guide to Emotional Agility. How to Use Soft Skills to Get Hard Results.** — Upper Saddle River, NJ.: FT Press, 2015.

6. Paul Ekman. **Emotions Revealed: Recognizing Faces and Feelings to Improve Communication and Emotional Life.** — NYC: Owl Books, 2007.

7. Vanessa Green Allen. **Me and My Feelings: A Kids' Guide to Understanding and Expressing Themselves.** — San Antonio, Texas: Althea Press, 2019.

8. Vyacheslav Dubynin. **Устройство и работа мозга (Brain Structure and the Way It Works)** / ПостНаука (PostNauka) // youtube.com [in Russian].

9. Kendra Cherry. **5 Reasons Emotions Are Important** // verywellmind.com

10. Tiago Forte. **How Emotions Are Made: The Theory of Constructed Emotion** // fortelabs.com

11. Tiffany Watt Smith. **The History of Human Emotions** // ted.com

12. Yale Center for Emotional Intelligence. **Mood Meter Overview** // youtube.com

13. Sophie Zadeh. **Are There Universal Expressions of Emotion?** // ted.com

Chapter 2. How Do I Know What I Am Feeling?

14. Karen Bluth. **The Self-Compassion Workbook for Teens: Mindfulness and Compassion Skills to Overcome Self-Criticism and Embrace Who You Are.** — Oakland, CA: Instant Help, 2017.

15. Kendra Cherry. **What Is the Negativity Bias?** // verywellmind.com

16. Mary Gavin. **The Power of Positive Emotions** // kidshealth.org

17. Alina Tugend. **Praise Is Fleeting, but Brickbats We Recall** // nytimes.com

18. **Where Are Emotions Felt in the Body? This Infographic Will Tell You** // greatist.com

Chapter 3. I Feel...

19. Lise Bourbeau. **Amour, Amour, Amour: la puissance de l'acceptation.** — Quebec City: ETC, 2007.

20. Sheri Van Dijk. **Don't Let Your Emotions Run Your Life for Teens.** — Oakland, CA: New Harbinger Pub., 2011.

21. Seth J. Gillihan. **Cognitive Behavioral Therapy Made Simple: 10 Strategies for Managing Anxiety, Depression, Anger, Panic, and Worry.** — San Antonio, TX: Althea Press, 2018.

22. Gretsov A. G., Popova E. G. **Исправь своё настроение сам (Fixing Your Own Spirits).** — St. Petersburg: Lesgaft National State University of Physical Education, Sport and Health, 2003 [in Russian].

23. Dan Dubravin. **Психология эмоций: чувства под контролем (Psychology of Emotions: Feelings Under Control).** — Kiev: IPIO, 2015 [in Russian].

24. Philip Zimbardo. **Shyness: What It Is, What To Do About It.** — Boston, MA: Da Capo Press, 1977.

25. Carroll Izard. **The Psychology of Emotions.** — NYC: Plenum, 1991.

26. Leone Milton, Marie Tomicic. **Ta makten — för att det funkar!** — Linkoping, Sweden: Olika Förlag, 2021.

27. Tara Brach. **Radical Acceptance: Embracing Your Life with the Heart of a Buddha.** — NYC: Random House Publishing Group, 2014.

28. Dr. Kristin Neff. **Self-Compassion: The Proven Power of Being Kind to Yourself.** — London: Hodder & Stoughton, 2011.

Chapter 4. Getting Along with Your Feelings

29. Dmitry Zhukov. **Биология поведения: гуморальные механизмы (Biology of Behavior: Humoral Mechanisms).** — St. Petersburg: Rech, 2004 [in Russian].

30. Eveline Crone. **Het sociale brein van de puber.** — Delft: Prometheus, 2012.

31. Ethan Kross. **Chatter. The Voice in Our Head, Why It Matters, and How to Harness It.** — London: Vermilion, 2021.

32. Marshall B. Rosenberg. **Nonviolent Communication: A Language of Life.** — Encinitas: Puddledancer Press, 1999.

33. Michael S. Sorensen. **I Hear You. The Surprisingly Simple Skill Behind Extraordinary Relationships.** — Saratoga Springs, UT: Autumn Creek Press, 2017.

34. Laurence Steinberg. **Age of Opportunity. Lesson from the New Science of Adolescence.** — Boston, MA: Houghton Mifflin Harcourt, 2014.

35. Daniel Siegel. **The Developing Mind: Toward a Neurobiology of Interpersonal Experience.** — New York: Guilford Press, 1999.

36. Editors of Teen Breathe. **Be Calm: Be Your Best Self Every Day (Be You).** — Lewes: Ammonite Press, 2019.

37. Tanya Richardson. **Zen Teen: 40 Ways to Stay Calm When Life Gets Stressful.** — Seal Press, 2018.

38. Daniel Siegel. **Brainstorm: The Power and Purpose of the Teenage Brain. Dr. Dan Siegel** // youtube.com

Chapter 5. What Do Others Feel?

39. Eric Berne. **Games People Play. The Psychology of Human Relationships.** — NYC: Grove Press, 1964.

40. Olga Gulevich. **Психология межгрупповых отношений (Psychology of Intergroup Relations).** — Moscow: MPSU, 2008 [in Russian].

41. Todd Nelson. **The Psychology of Prejudice.** — Boston, MA: Allyn and Bacon, 2005.

42. Kerry Patterson, Joseph Grenny, Ron McMillan, and Al Switzler. **Crucial Conversation: Tools for Talking When Stakes Are High.** — NYC: McGraw Hill Professional, 2011.

43. Robert Sapolsky. **Behave: The Biology of Humans at Our Best and Worst.** — London: Penguin Press, 2017.

44. Douglas Stone, Sheila Heen. **Thanks for the Feedback: The Science and Art of Receiving Feedback Well.** — NYC: Viking, 2014.

45. Sam Harris. **Lying.** — Los Angeles, CA: Four Elephants Press, 2011.

46. Roger Fisher, William L. Uri, Bruce Patton. **Getting to Yes. Negotiating Agreement Without Giving In.** — London: Penguin Group, 1991.

47. Gary Chapman. **The Five Love Languages.** — Chicago: Northfield Pub., 1992.

48. Christian Picciolini. **My Descent into America's Neo-Nazi Movement and How I Got Out** // ted.com

An educational visual book for children of middle/high school age and young adults

EMOTIONS FOR TEENS AND TWEENS
The first visual book on emotional intelligence for tweens and teens told through infographics.
A graphic guide to understanding, managing, expressing feelings, and building relationships

Creator of original concept and editor-in-chief *Maria Gorina*
Responsible for publishing *Yulia Antipova*
Language editors *Laird Cenotto, Todd Jackson, Natalia Erokhina*
Translated by *Laird Cenotto*

For more information contact:
ivigreen.com
hello@ivigreen.com

ISBN 978-5-6045240-2-2

Made in the USA
Las Vegas, NV
16 December 2024

14285908R00064